Contents

PROFILES

Evgeni Malkin 30
Sidney Crosb 48
Dan Bylsm 56
Bill Guerin 66
'The Genos' 96

KEY STORIES/PRESEASON

Ground broken on new arena site 6
Whitney undergoes left foot surgery 8
Malkin considered for alternate captain 10
Gonchar suffers shoulder injury 12
Penguins leave for season-opening trip to Sweden 14
Gonchar to miss at least four months 16

REGULAR-SEASON

Season-opening win over Ottawa in Stockholm 18
Home-opener loss to New Jersey 20
Crosby and Malkin reach milestones in win 22
Sykora, Dupuis collect first career hat tricks 24
Ryan Whitney returns to lineup from injury 26
Penguins, Oilers swap backup goaltenders 28
Bylsma replaces Therrien as head coach 34
Bylsma gets first victory as NHL coach 38
Whitney traded to Anaheim for Kunitz and Tangradi .. 40
Kunitz scores in first game as a Penguin 42
Pens acquire Guerin and Adams at trade deadline ... 44
Crosby returns from four-game absence 46
Malkin posts five points to open up lead in scoring race . 52
Penguins clinch playoff berth with win at Tampa Bay ... 54
Penguins get fourth seed in East, draw Flyers in Round 1 ... 62

POST SEASON/FIRST ROUND

Guerin scores overtime winner in Game 2 64
Fleury makes 45 saves in Game 3 70
Pens rally from 3-0 deficit to win Game 6, eliminate Flyers 72
Interim tag removed from Bylsma's title 74

SECOND ROUND

Crosby, Ovechkin record dueling hat tricks in Game 2 76
Malkin responds to critics in Game 3; Letang scores in OT 78
Malkin gets overtime winner in Game 5 80
Crosby sparks Game 7 blowout at Washington 82

EASTERN CONFERENCE FINAL

Malkin dominates third period in Game 2 84
Pens sweep Hurricanes for Eastern Conference title 86

STANLEY CUP FINAL

Red Wings strike first with win on home ice 88
Penguins fall to Wings in Game 2 90
Home ice lifts Penguins to victory in Game 3 92
Penguins even series at 2-2 with another home win 94
Red Wings dominate Penguins in Game 5 100
Third line lifts Penguins in Game 6 win 102
Penguins hoist Stanley Cup after 2-1 win in Game 7 104
Penguins fans celebrate in Detroit 106
Game 7 celebration spills onto Pittsburgh streets 108
Penguins players share their Stanley Cup thoughts 110
Championship parade draws 375,000 fans downtown 112

The Penguins' **Sergei Gonchar** sits in the locker room with his daughter after the Penguins beat the Red Wings in Game 7 of the Stanley Cup Final.

Chaz Palla/Trib Total Media

Foreword

Lord Stanley's Cup is back where Mario Lemieux says "it belongs."

Returning it to Pittsburgh for a third time — and first since Lemieux won it as a player in 1992 — required a journey along a bumpy, hilly and often slippery road. The Penguins, though, always believed that road was paved with silver.

Their story started in July 2008 when, just weeks after a gut-wrenching loss in the Stanley Cup Final, the Penguins started losing players from that team on a daily basis. In all, six forwards did not return, including star winger Marian Hossa, who opted to play for the same Detroit Red Wings that denied the Penguins the Cup.

By the time the regular season opened with a 10-day trip to Europe, the Penguins were well on their way toward a tumultuous season. Top defensemen Ryan Whitney and Sergei Gonchar were hurt, and the reconfigured roster was struggling to score.

By Feb. 15, all hope for a return to the Cup Final seemed lost. The club was 10th in the Eastern Conference, five points from a playoff spot and now under the stewardship of Dan Bylsma, a first-year AHL coach who replaced Michel Therrien.

Any Penguins fan is well aware how the story went from there.

Cup-winning wingers Chris Kunitz, Bill Guerin and Craig Adams arrived. Gonchar returned from injury and to his sure-handed form. Centers Evgeni Malkin and Sidney Crosby reminded the hockey world that they are its best 1-2 punch.

Goalie Marc-Andre Fleury made all the big saves, and role-playing forwards Jordan Staal, Tyler Kennedy and Max Talbot combined with heart-and-soul defensemen Brooks Orpik and Rob Scuderi to provide the Penguins with all the necessary ingredients for another Cup run.

This one ended with an epic Final, won in seven games by the Penguins who along their playoff journey denied the Cup to their archrivals (the Flyers), Crosby's chief nemesis (Capitals winger Alex Ovechkin), Staal's brother (Hurricanes center Eric), and Hossa's Red Wings.

Bringing back the Cup was anything but easy for the Penguins. Don't take our word, though — this collection of Tribune-Review articles tells the story of the team's roller-coaster season as we covered it.

Enjoy,
Rob Rossi
Trib Total Media Penguins beat reporter

NEW ARENA GR

The ceremony took pla
The arena is scheduled to open in ti

GROUNDBREAKING
Thursday, August 14
for the 2010-2011 hockey season

Pittsburgh Penguins owner **Mario Lemieux** discusses the groundbreaking of the $290 million multi-purpose Consol Center that will sit along Centre Avenue in the Hill District and replace the Mellon Arena.

Pittsburgh Penguins team officials and elected leaders participate in the groundbreaking of the new Consol Center. (From left) Penguins president **David Morehouse**, Allegheny County Chief Executive **Dan Onorato**, Penguins owner **Mario Lemieux**, Pittsburgh Mayor **Luke Ravenstahl**, Penguins CEO **Ken Sawyer** and Governor **Edward G. Rendell**.

Penguins defenseman **Ryan Whitney** said he played most of the 2007-08 season on one healthy foot.

PENS' WHITNEY OUT AT LEAST THREE MONTHS

By Rob Rossi/TRIB TOTAL MEDIA

○ ○ ○ ○ ○

Saturday, August 16, 2008

Ryan Whitney's critics have considerably less ammunition today.

Turns out, the defenseman skated on one healthy foot last season.

Whitney, whose point total dropped from 59 in 2006-07 to 40 in 2007-08, underwent surgery to correct a left-foot misalignment Friday in Charlotte. Full recovery from the procedure, an osteotomy, usually takes three to five months.

"I just couldn't live on one healthy foot anymore, let alone try to skate," Whitney said, on the eve of his surgery. "We've tried everything to avoid surgery because we knew it would mean missing a chunk of the season. But nothing worked."

Whitney, entering the second season of a six-year, $24 million contract he signed in July 2007, said general manager Ray Shero and coach Michel Therrien "were stunned" during season-ending meetings when Whitney informed them he had played all of last season on basically one skate.

Whitney said several teammates, including defenseman Brooks Orpik and center Sidney Crosby, were aware his left foot "was in bad shape" last season, but he didn't want an injury to be an excuse for an admittedly disappointing season.

"I'm not making that an excuse," Whitney said. "I need to perform better than I did, and I know that is the expectation. But I've always thought skating was the biggest part of my game, and last season, I couldn't skate like I can."

Whitney's loss deals a blow to the Penguins. He spent much of the past two seasons working the point on the power play, where he tallied 16 of his 26 goals.

The Penguins, however, are deep on defense. They will open training camp next month with seven healthy defensemen that are NHL-tested, and right-handed shooting Kris Letang could ease the temporary loss of Whitney.

Also, the organization's top prospect, defenseman Alex Goligoski, starred with Wilkes-Barre of the AHL during his first professional year last season.

Whitney said he first noticed his foot pain when the Penguins played the Ottawa Senators in the opening round of the 2007 Stanley Cup playoffs. He worked with team trainers to correct the problem prior to and during last season, but none of the suggested methods — specifically the use of orthotics — worked.

The Penguins supported his decision to seek several medical opinions before opting for surgery, Whitney said. He visited three orthopedic specialists this summer, each of whom initially recommended more conservative treatment options.

But each of those physicians ultimately recommended the osteotomy procedure.

Whitney said missing a portion of the season "looked like a certainty" after consulting with a North Carolina physician who performed the surgery.

"Obviously, had we known surgery was inevitable, we would have had it in June," Whitney said. "Ray was great about trying to treat this without surgery, but nothing we tried worked.

"It's frustrating. We went from being optimistic, I wouldn't miss any time, to maybe not coming back until January. But at least now I know when I come back this year, it will be the me that's coming back."

Ryan Whitney first noticed his foot pain when the Penguins played the Ottawa Senators in the opening round of the 2007 playoffs.

MALKIN 'A' TRUE LEADER FOR PENGUINS

By Rob Rossi/TRIB TOTAL MEDIA

Sunday, September 21, 2008

You can't spell Malkin without an "A."

Calling him "one of our leaders," coach Michel Therrien said Saturday center Evgeni Malkin "definitely" is under consideration to serve as an alternate captain this season — a move that would have the endorsement of captain Sidney Crosby.

"He's a great candidate, and we're going to help him," Therrien said before the Penguins played Tampa Bay in their exhibition home opener — the first contest at Mellon Arena since Game 6 of the Stanley Cup final.

"We know (Malkin's) potential ... not only as a player, but as a leader, too."

When Therrien replaced Eddie Olczyk as coach Dec. 15, 2005, he immediately named Crosby an alternate captain. That move drew criticism. But Crosby prospered from the increased responsibility and believes a similar circumstance for Malkin would be the right move.

"I think so," Crosby said. "He's a guy that we're going to depend on a lot. If he's the guy that gets a responsibility like that, it's well-deserved."

Therrien said he will take the remainder of training camp to reach a decision on what player — or possibly players — will replace departed left wing Ryan Malone as an alternate captain. But Malkin, 22, who signed a five-year extension worth $43.5 million over the summer, is on the short list of contenders.

Malkin, second in MVP voting and the scoring race last season, said yesterday the time is not right to become an alternate captain.

"There are more people, older ... not me, no way," Malkin said. "Maybe a couple years more. I need to speak English."

Malkin, whose first language is Russian, is still not comfortable speaking English. But teammates such as defensemen Brooks Orpik and fellow Russian and alternate captain Sergei Gonchar insist Malkin is fluent enough to handle primary responsibilities of an alternate — officially to speak with on-ice officials, unofficially to deal with the media.

"Maybe the language would be a little bit of a problem in the beginning," Gonchar said. "But I do believe he's getting better. He's more comfortable. He's going to speak more and more (this season). It's kind of (a) natural (progression)."

Gonchar added that making Malkin an alternate captain is "worth considering ... if you look at the picture long-term."

"At this point, he may not feel it's the right decision yet," Gonchar said. "If you look at the situation, for the team's well-being, it's going to help him to develop into a better player and be more responsible."

Crosby, 18 when he donned an "A" as a rookie, said receiving the letter "probably added a little bit of responsibility."

"I think it made me better," Crosby said.

Forward Max Talbot, who roomed with Malkin for road trips last season, described him as "definitely a leader on this team."

"It's not by talking, but by acting," Talbot said. "He's always there in the big moments."

Malkin morphed from a willing sidekick to Crosby into a dominant offensive centerpiece after Crosby was injured with a right high-ankle sprain Jan. 18. Over the final 36 games of the regular 07-08 season, Malkin scored 24 goals and recorded 54 points to finish with 47 goals and 106 points.

He scored seven goals and recorded 17 points in the Penguins' opening 10 playoff games, but registered just two goals and five points over their final 10 postseason contests — including only a goal and two assists in the Stanley Cup final.

Orpik, a close Malkin confidant, said the Penguins would never have reached the final without Malkin's mature performance during a mostly Crosby-less final two months of the regular season.

"Guys, especially when Sid was down last year, definitely looked at him to, I wouldn't say carry us, but he definitely was a leader up front," Orpik said.

"It's something I think he takes upon himself. He might not be vocal, but I think he kind of likes it, to be honest — being a leader of the team and taking that starring role."

Penguins center **Evgeni Malkin** could benefit from the added responsibility if he is named alternate captain.

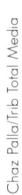

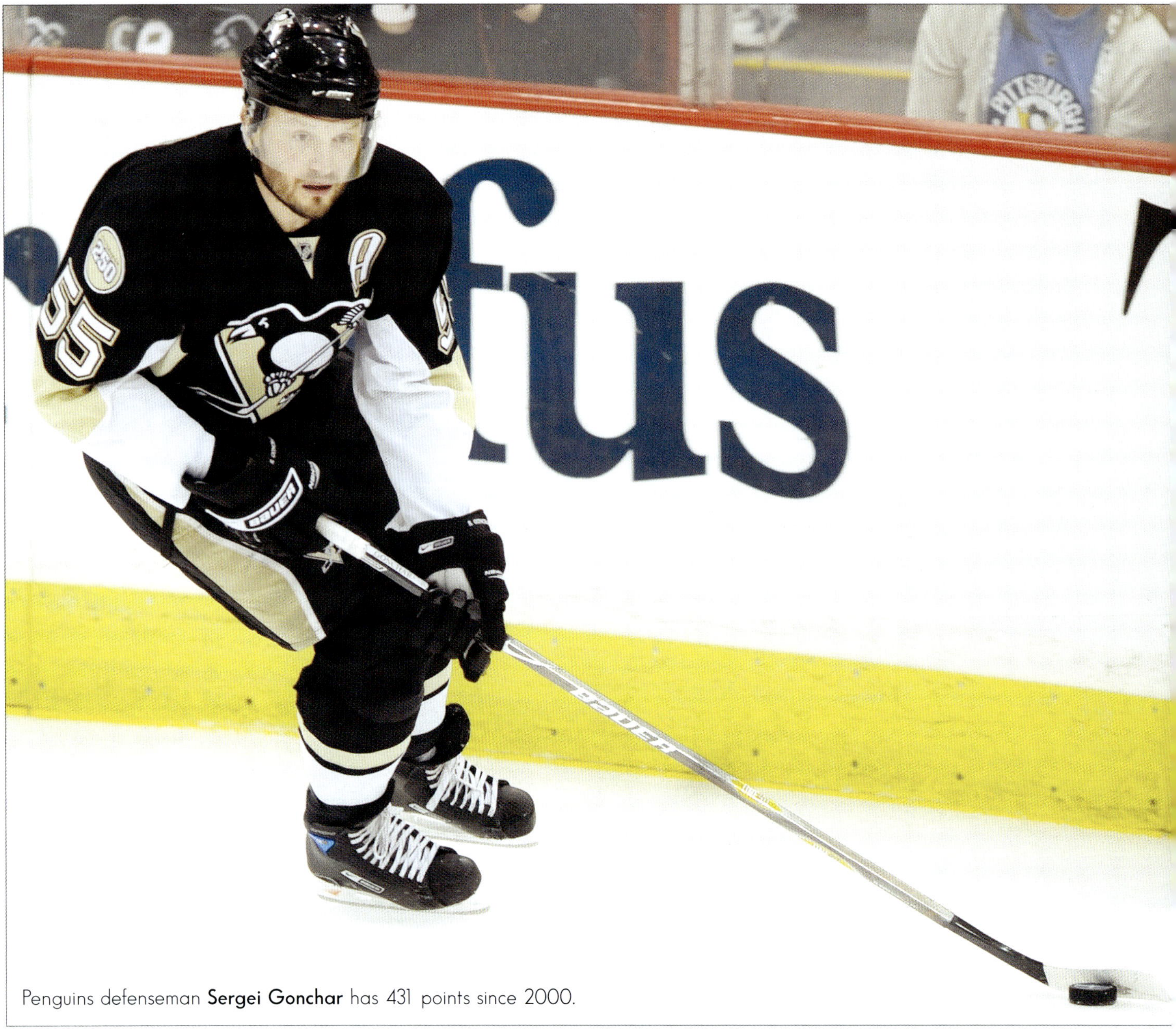

Chaz Palla/Trib Total Media

Penguins defenseman **Sergei Gonchar** has 431 points since 2000.

DISLOCATED SHOULDER SIDELINES GONCHAR

By Rob Rossi/TRIB TOTAL MEDIA

Thursday, September 25, 2008

The Penguins won't have their "Sarge" running the show for a while.

Top defenseman Sergei Gonchar is out indefinitely with a left shoulder dislocation — the result of a hit into the boards by Tampa Bay forward David Koci midway through the opening period of an exhibition game Saturday at Mellon Arena.

General manager Ray Shero said Wednesday "indefinite is really the way to put it, because we don't know."

"We won't know more maybe until next week, when he has a chance to see some other doctors, get some other opinions, other avenues he can take for getting better," Shero said prior to the Penguins' final home exhibition game against Toronto. "Right now, he's starting his rehab."

Gonchar has yet to undergo a Magnetic Resonance Imaging examination, Shero said. He added that surgery "is an option" and said the organization would support Gonchar if he sought that option.

Gonchar, 34, was not available for comment.

J.P. Barry, who represents Gonchar, said via a text message he had "no idea yet" how much time Gonchar might miss.

"We are still getting all the advice we need on the best course of action," Barry wrote.

The loss of Gonchar, the NHL's second-highest scoring defenseman with 431 points since 2000, is a jarring blow to the Penguins — especially considering the current status of defenseman Ryan Whitney.

An August surgery to correct a left-foot deformity will keep Whitney out until at least December. Gonchar (132) and Whitney (99) have combined to account for 71 percent of the Penguins' defensive scoring the past two seasons.

Gonchar has worked the point on the Penguins' top power-play unit since his arrival for the 2005-06 season. He has scored 26 goals and recorded 106 assists for an advantage attack that finished no lower than sixth over that span.

Assistant coach Mike Yeo, who runs the club's power play, said Sunday that Whitney "would have been the obvious replacement for Gonchar" on that unit. Whitney has scored 20 goals and recorded 53 assists on the power play the past three seasons.

The Penguins placed center Evgeni Malkin on the power-play point last night, with rookie defenseman Alex Goligoski working the off-point that Malkin occupied late last season.

Goligoski, a dominant offensive player over three seasons at the University of Minnesota (98 points in 117 games), had a standout first professional season last year. He scored 10 goals and recorded 38 points in 70 regular-season games with AHL affiliate Wilkes-Barre — adding four goals and 28 points in 23 Calder Cup playoff contests.

Coach Michel Therrien said the injuries to Gonchar and Whitney "provided opportunities for young players to prove they belong in the NHL." He was specifically referring to Goligoski and right-handed shooting defenseman Kris Letang, who scored six goals and recorded 17 points over 63 games with the Penguins last season.

Letang's performance forced veteran Darryl Sydor to watch most of the Stanley Cup playoffs as a healthy scratch. However, Sydor replaced Letang after Game 2 of the Stanley Cup final.

Goligoski, 23, and Letang, 21, were by far the youngest defensemen competing in training camp for a spot among the Penguins' top six. They are joined by veterans Brooks Orpik, 27, Rob Scuderi, 29, Hal Gill, 33, and Sydor, 36.

Orpik and Gonchar were considered the club's top defensive pairing. Gonchar paced the club with a per-game average ice time of 25 minutes and 54 seconds last season.

Shero termed playing without Gonchar and Whitney — third in average ice time last season at 22:26 — "a challenge," but added "it's no different than last year playing without your top goaltender and top player."

Center Sidney Crosby and goalie Marc-Andre Fleury each missed significant time last season due to ankle sprains. The Penguins still won the Atlantic Division — their first division title since 1998.

"As I've said about this team, it's been very resilient," Shero said. "We do have some younger players that certainly deserve the opportunity to step up and play, and we do have some veterans that can step up as well.

"Three weeks ago we were happy with our depth on defense, and right now I'm happy we have that."

There's no 'O' in defense

The Penguins will start the season without defensemen Sergei Gonchar and Ryan Whitney, who combined for 71 percent of the points provided from that position the past two seasons. A look at the offensive production of the club's current defensemen over that span:

Player	G	A	Pts
Sergei Gonchar	25	107	132
Ryan Whitney	26	73	99
*Hal Gill	9	35	44
#Darryl Sydor	6	28	34
Kris Letang	8	11	19
Brooks Orpik	1	16	17
Rob Scuderi	1	15	16
Mark Eaton	0	6	6
^Alex Goligoski	0	2	2
Danny Richmond	0	2	2

*8 goals, 32 assists, 40 points with Toronto (2006-2008)
#5 goals, 16 assists, 21 points with Dallas (2006-07)
^Appeared in 3 games (2007-08); would be a rookie this season

Source: NHL, Pittsburgh Penguins

PENS HOPE STOCKHOLM TRIP ENHANCES TEAM CHEMISTRY

By Rob Rossi/TRIB TOTAL MEDIA

○ ○ ○ ○ ○

Sunday, September 28, 2008

Spending nine of the next 10 days in Stockholm has Penguins of all nationalities excited.

The Czech: "It's a beautiful city," left wing Petr Sykora said. "It's expensive. So expensive I cannot afford to live there. But it's beautiful. There's nothing like it."

The American: "It's incredible," general manager Ray Shero said. "There's so much to see. You walk around, and I think you can actually feel the history."

The Ukrainian: "It's wonderful," left wing Ruslan Fedotenko said. "You have to see it. Then you can't help but love everything about it."

The Canadian: "It's gonna be a great opportunity for the newcomers and the guys from last year to get a chance to get to know each other a lot better," coach Michel Therrien said. "That's what I want to see in Stockholm."

Spoken like a man on a mission to return the Stanley Cup to Pittsburgh for the first time since 1992.

Therrien knows that an opportunity to "be a winner," as the Penguins' 2008-09 motto demands, must start with statement-making performances Oct. 4 and 5 against Ottawa at Globe Arena in Stockholm, a city that professes to "live life to its fullest."

That is exactly what Therrien and Shero want from the Penguins on this European trip.

"It's not all about hockey," Shero said. "It's such a hectic start to training camp, but the trip itself is real good. I'd say it's beneficial for us. We've got other things on the agenda besides fly, eat and practice.

"It's going to be a good bonding experience for everybody, especially the players."

With few mandatory team activities scheduled, Shero wants the Penguins to come together on their own.

No matter how, the Penguins need to come together — right now.

They are down six of 12 forwards that played at least one game in the Cup final. Marian Hossa (Detroit), Ryan Malone, Adam Hall and Gary Roberts (Tampa Bay), Jarkko Ruutu (Ottawa) and Georges Laraque (Montreal) left a void with their off-season departures.

The players acquired to replace them — Fedotenko, Miroslav Satan, Matt Cooke, Janne Pesonen and Eric Godard — have had few days to connect with the young nucleus of those mostly responsible for a dramatic two-year turnaround from bottom dweller to championship contender.

Therrien knew entering August a lot would ride on those players' ability to fit with a tight-knit team. That was before long-term injuries to defensemen Ryan Whitney (left foot) and Sergei Gonchar (left shoulder) added to the altered feel in the dressing room.

"You can't replace the guys we lost over the summer, just like you can't replace Whitney and Gonchar," Therrien said. "But we have a good, proud group of young players. This is when you look to (captain) Sidney Crosby and (defenseman) Brooks Orpik and (center Max) Talbot — guys that are leaders now."

Orpik said Europe might be the place the Penguins come together.

"We have a group here that gets along really well," Orpik said. "You see a lot of older guys come here from other teams and you hear them say it — how lucky (we) are to have this kind of group because it's not like that at other places."

The competitive spirits of Crosby and fellow superstar center Evgeni Malkin set the tone for new players, defenseman Hal Gill said. Gill picked up quickly on "the tight team bond" upon his arrival last February after a trade from Toronto.

"Chemistry is a funny thing — you can't make it," Gill said. "But between 'Geno' and Sid, they both want to be

Penguins defenseman **Brooks Orpik** (left) and teammate **Matt Cooke** take in the sights during the team's trip to Stockholm, Sweden.

the go-to guy, and they compete with each other, and that spreads throughout the room. If Mark (Eaton) is pushing me, and I'm pushing him, that's a good thing, and that's the kind of chemistry you need."

Satan, expected to fill the role as right wing for Crosby that Hossa vacated, noticed "a very natural chemistry" among the Penguins during player-run skating sessions at Southpointe before training camp.

"It was right away, and it was obvious — the feeling that this is a team, not just great individual players, and the best guys are the guys working hardest in practice," Satan said. "I haven't been on that kind of team before. It makes you want to keep up with them, work harder than you did before, because you want to fit in."

Fedotenko said this trip will only expedite the new players' assimilation into the fabric the franchise stalwarts have woven.

"Long road trips usually are good to get close to one another," he said. "You're away from the distractions, and there are a lot of them when you are new — getting the house ready, learning the neighborhood, where to eat.

"But I've had guys giving me advice on that since I signed with (the Penguins). This organization makes you feel at home right away."

PENGUINS MARCHING ON WITHOUT 'SARGE' IN LINEUP

By Rob Rossi/TRIB TOTAL MEDIA

○ ○ ○ ○ ○

Wednesday, October 1, 2008

STOCKHOLM, Sweden — Time, likely the next six months, will tell just how much defenseman Sergei Gonchar means to the Penguins.

Gonchar will undergo arthroscopic surgery Thursday in Pittsburgh to repair a dislocated left shoulder. Noted specialist Dr. Mark Rodosky will perform a procedure necessary to repair cartilage and ligament damage.

The Penguins made the announcement Tuesday after several media outlets, including Trib Total Media, reported Gonchar's impending surgery Monday.

Gonchar, injured on a hard hit by Tampa Bay forward David Koci during the first period of the Penguins' exhibition opener Sept. 20, will miss at least four months. Full recovery could cost him six months, though the Penguins expect him to return sometime in March.

His absence from the lineup will provide quite a challenge for the Penguins, who are down their top two defensemen in terms of points and minutes from last season. Ryan Whitney, second to Gonchar in both categories, is out until December recovering from left foot surgery in August.

Neither Gonchar nor Whitney accompanied the Penguins on a season-opening European trip.

No less an authority on value than former league MVP Sidney Crosby has called Gonchar hockey's "most underrated player."

"You don't expect (significant injuries) two years in a row," said Crosby, who along with goaltender Marc-Andre Fleury missed nearly 30 games last season due to a right high ankle sprain. "It's never easy. It's a good challenge, though, for guys who are going to get an opportunity to come in and get a bigger role."

Those guys include defensemen Alex Goligoski, a rookie, and Darryl Sydor, the Penguins' player with the most NHL experience. They've gone from fighting for a top-six spot at the start of camp to being potentially key components for a defensive corps with less certainty than it had Aug. 1.

Kris Letang, a promising right-handed shooter, finished his rookie campaign as a healthy scratch in the last four games of the Stanley Cup final. Mark Eaton missed the entire second half due to a torn right anterior cruciate ligament.

"We're going to need all hands on deck," general manager Ray Shero said.

Defensemen **Darryl Sydor** (left) and **Alex Goligoski** (right) figure to get more playing time with the loss of Sergei Gonchar.

Penguins defenseman **Sergei Gonchar** has been referred to by Sidney Crosby as hockey's 'most underrated player.'

Penguins forward **Tyler Kennedy** celebrates with teammate **Kris Letang** after scoring the winning goal against Ottawa during the season opener in Stockholm, Sweden.

UNLIKELY SOURCES POWER PENS TO VICTORY

By Rob Rossi/TRIB TOTAL MEDIA

○○○○○

Sunday, October 5, 2008

STOCKHOLM, Sweden — Cocky is not a word most people associate with right wing Tyler Kennedy.

Quiet describes him best.

Still, Kennedy's road roommate, left wing Jordan Staal, knew he was in for a long night Saturday after Kennedy scored twice yesterday — the Penguins' first and last goals — in a rousing 4-3 overtime victory over the Ottawa Senators at Globe Arena in the NHL Premier series.

"Trust me, you'll see it if you room with him," Staal said of Kennedy's until now unknown boastful side. "He's always got something to say.

"You don't want to say cocky, but he's definitely a confident person, and he plays like that. It's great to see."

It certainly was great for the Penguins, who managed to earn two points despite failing to convert on seven power-play opportunities.

The Big Three played a part in this season-opening win.

Goaltender Marc-Andre Fleury stopped 32 of 35 shots, including all 13 after the second period.

Center Evgeni Malkin capped a shorthanded breakaway with a highlight-reel goal off his backhand in the second period.

Captain Sidney Crosby, visibly frustrated by his club's power-play struggles entering the second intermission, assisted on a goal early in the third that pulled the Penguins even, 3-3.

But yesterday belonged to Kennedy, who seconds into the game snapped a 29-game goal drought, including the playoffs, that dated to March 16.

Of course, Kennedy's winning-goal with 25 seconds remaining in overtime could not have come to pass had defenseman Rob Scuderi not converted a cross-ice pass from Crosby — as sharp as it was daring — into a tying tally at 3:56 of the third period.

"The play was all Sid, he really moved the goalie side-to-side," said Scuderi, who had not scored since Feb. 16, 2007. "I just tried to put it on net and let something happen."

Here's what happened: Without the services of defensemen Sergei Gonchar (left shoulder) and Ryan Whitney (left foot) — players that have accounted for 71 percent of the Penguins' defensive point production the past two seasons — Scuderi, without a goal in 120 games, including the playoffs, provided Crosby his first point of the season.

"That was kind of a long shot," coach Michel Therrien said. "We weren't expecting that one coming."

Upon cradling Crosby's pass, Scuderi heard "an alarm go off in (his) head."

"Sometimes it's a little scary ... when I'm below the top of the circles," Scuderi said. "But I knew I was going to shoot it. (Crosby had) moved everybody over to his side and slid it over.

"It was a great play by him."

It was a great day for Kennedy, whose confidence entering training camp seemed curious given the scoring struggles to end his rookie campaign last season.

But armed with a two-year extension, inked last week, and a spot on a scoring line with Staal and Malkin, Kennedy eased any pain that could have been felt by right wing Petr Sykora's injury-related scratch.

He pumped his right arm after his first goal, (and) capped his second with a turnaround mad-dash toward a mob of celebrating teammates.

"The first one, I was glad to get (the proverbial monkey) off my back," Kennedy said. "The second, I was just excited to help the team win."

Those are not exactly the words of a cocky roommate.

But the Penguins' Mr. Kennedy figures he has a long way to go before he's a regular main-event performer like, say, Staal.

"He's got a lot more rank than I do," Kennedy said.

Season opens with win in Stockholm

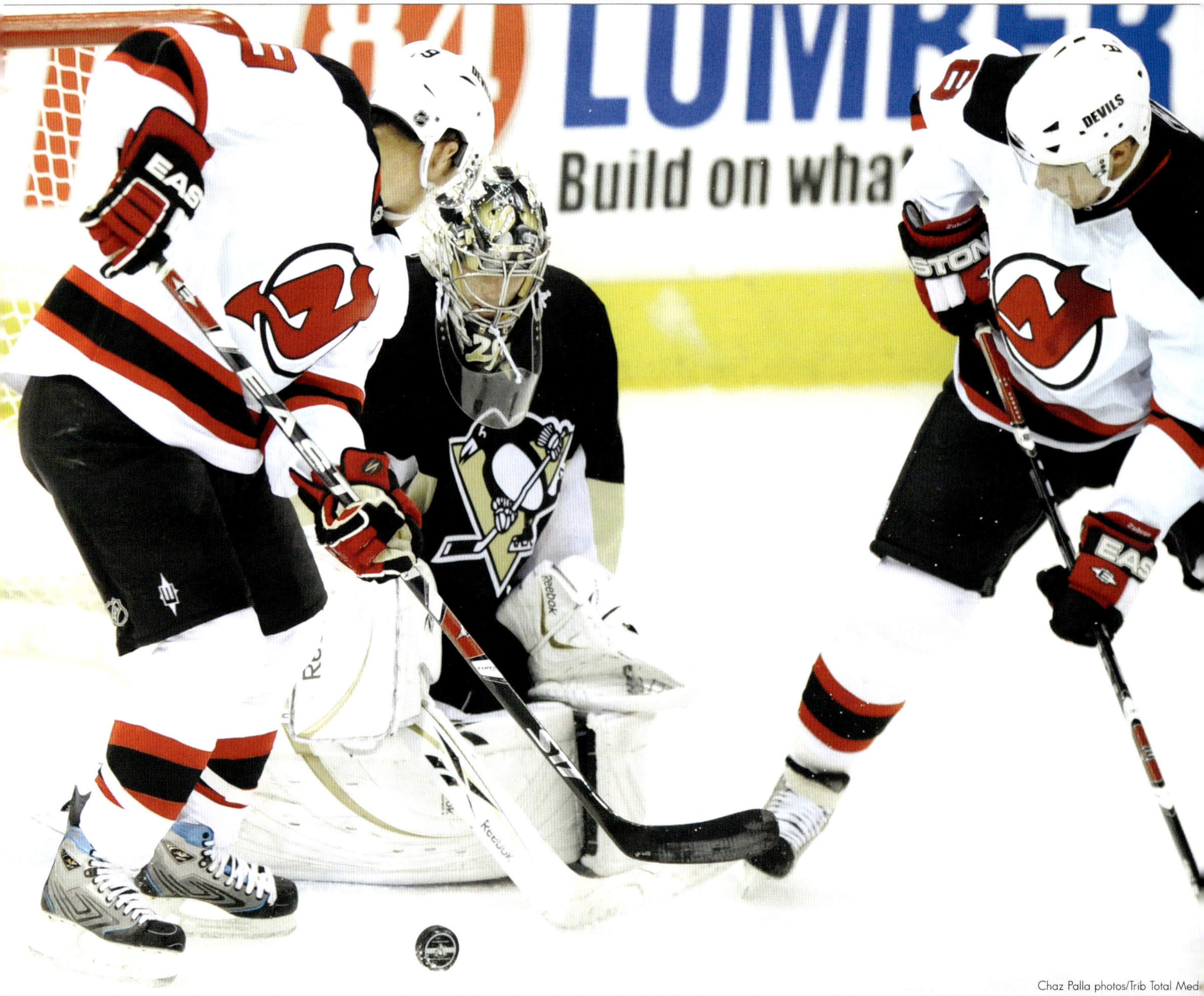

Chaz Palla photos/Trib Total Med

Penguins goaltender **Marc-Andre Fleury** makes a second-period save on the Devils' Zach Parise.

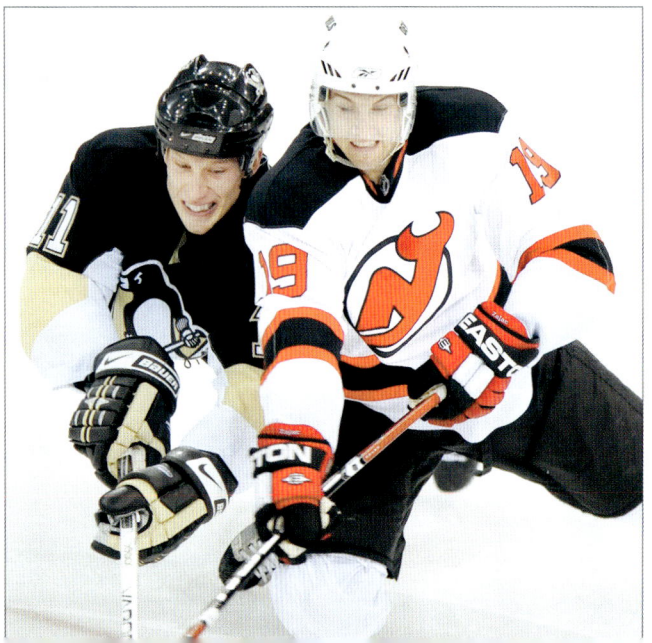

(Left) Penguins center **Jordan Staal** and Devils center Travis Zajac fight for the puck in the second period.

(Right) Devils center Travis Zajac celebrates Zach Parise's game-winning goal at 4:22 of overtime.

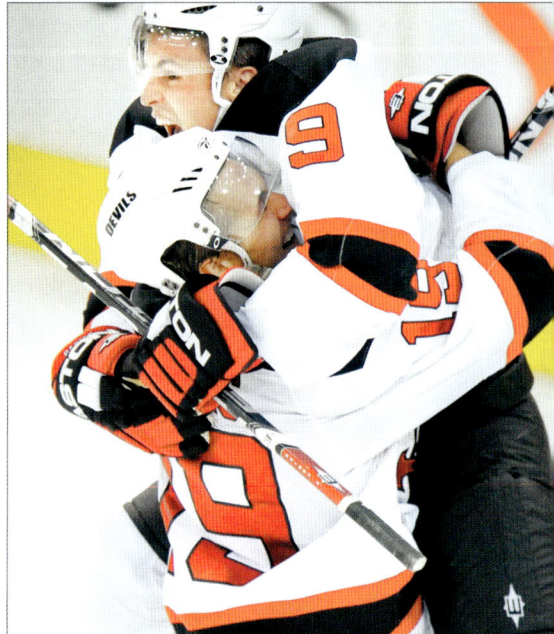

FLEURY'S EXCELLENCE CAN'T BAIL OUT PENGUINS

By Rob Rossi/TRIB TOTAL MEDIA

○ ○ ○ ○ ○

Sunday, October 12, 2008

Their "Flower" in mid-October bloom prevented the Penguins' home opener from becoming a total disaster.

Still, even a 47-save performance Saturday by goaltender Marc-Andre Fleury against the New Jersey Devils at Mellon Arena could not mask the obvious.

"We didn't deserve a win," Penguins captain Sidney Crosby said following a disappointing 2-1 overtime loss to the Devils. "We didn't deserve a point."

Fleury, though, deserved better than an overtime loss.

He had turned aside 44 shots before New Jersey left wing Patrik Elias sent a puck cross-ice and toward the cage late in the third period.

Youth hockey players note: What follows is the perfect example why sending pucks near the net is never a bad idea, especially when trailing by a goal.

The Devils, down 1-0 at the time of Elias' desperation shot, benefited from a lucky carom off defenseman Hal Gill's right boot. The puck, which would have sailed past the slot clean, bounced off that skate and behind Fleury with 2:29 remaining in regulation.

New Jersey won the game 4:22 into overtime on left wing Zach Parise's goal.

Final shot total: Devils 49, Penguins ...

"Fifteen," defenseman Mark Eaton said. "Not a good effort."

The Penguins registered only seven shots over the final 44:22.

"We had a great first period," Eaton said. "But for some reason, after that, we got away from our game of putting pucks behind (the Devils' defense) and making them go the length of the ice."

Penguins coach Michel Therrien, who praised Fleury for "giving (the Penguins) a point," said simply that his team "didn't work."

"It's pretty simple," Therrien said. "New Jersey played an outstanding game ... (was) extremely hard on us. The result is what we saw."

Fleury saw no reason to pay homage to his individual effort after a defeat, even if his performance upstaged boyhood hockey idol and New Jersey goaltender Martin Brodeur.

"My job is to make the saves," Fleury said. "(This game) was like that. But other nights it is me who doesn't get any shots and it's our guys getting shots on the other side."

The Penguins could not capitalize on a shot of energy provided by right wing Miroslav Satan, who scored his first goal of the season — on his fourth shot — at 11:52 of the opening period.

Satan, signed as a free agent over the summer to offset the departure of right wing Marian Hossa, made New Jersey right wing Brian Gionta pay for a hooking penalty.

It was the Penguins' second power-play goal in 15 chances. They are 2 for 18 with the advantage this season.

They are also 1-1-1 with 3 points — not exactly the start they expected coming off a Stanley Cup final trip last season.

"It's extremely disappointing," Eaton said.

Penguins captain **Sidney Crosby** scores his 100th career goal, 200th career assist, and 300th career point during the same game in which center **Evgeni Malkin** scores his 200th career point.

DYNAMIC DUO SHINES IN PENS' 4-1 VICTORY

By Rob Rossi/TRIB TOTAL MEDIA

○ ○ ○ ○ ○

Sunday, October 19, 2008

Comic books have Batman and Robin. Comedians have Dean Martin and Jerry Lewis. Pop music has John Lennon and Paul McCartney.

The Penguins have centers Sidney Crosby and Evgeni Malkin — a dynamic duo that may ultimately rate with the all-time greats.

As modern 1-2 punches go, they have few equals in the NHL.

Skating regular shifts as linemates for the first time this season Saturday, Crosby and Malkin fueled a sigh-of-relief 4-1 victory against the Toronto Maple Leafs at Mellon Arena.

"I expect leadership," coach Michel Therrien said before the game of the Crosby-Malkin pairing.

"The Kid" and "Geno" delivered that and, more importantly, on the score sheet with four points each.

A 71st-consecutive sellout crowd watched, as Crosby and Malkin assisted on left winger Pascal Dupuis' first-period goal, his second, and a power-play tally by Miroslav Satan, his third, in the second period.

Crosby earned his 200th NHL assist on Dupuis' goal and 300th point on Satan's tally.

He added his 100th goal in the third period to ice the victory. Malkin assisted for his 200th point.

They each assisted on right wing Petr Sykora's goal late in the third.

The Penguins improved to 3-2-1 with 7 points. They went 2-1-1 on a four-game home stand that followed a season-opening two-game series against Ottawa in Stockholm, Sweden.

Goaltender Marc-Andre Fleury was strong once again, turning aside 26 shots. He has allowed only nine goals on 136 shots at home.

"He's been great for us," center Jordan Staal said. "You can't say enough about 'Flower.'"

Greg Shamus photos/Pittsburgh Penguins

Penguins winger **Petr Sykora** celebrates his first career hat trick with Sidney Crosby.

SYKORA, DUPUIS POWER PENGUINS

By Tricia Lafferty/TRIB TOTAL MEDIA

○ ○ ○ ○ ○

Friday, December 12, 2008

It's definitely one of those nights when Petr Sykora nets a hat trick. Same goes for Penguins teammate Pascal Dupuis.

Actually, it had never been one of those nights ... until Thursday.

Sykora and Dupuis tallied their first NHL hat tricks in the Penguins' 9-2 victory over the New York Islanders at Mellon Arena.

"I'm so happy for him," Sykora said of Dupuis. "I can kind of relate to that feeling of the first hat trick."

Scoring three goals in a game had proven tricky for Sykora. A sharp-shooting right wing now with 285 goals to his credit, he had amassed a record 38 two-goal games without recording a hat trick.

He dodged a 39th at 15:42 of the second period last night. Unguarded in the slot, Sykora one-touched a pass from center Sidney Crosby past backup New York goalie Yann Danis for his 10th goal of the season.

"As much as I didn't want to (say), it did bother me," said Sykora of his hat trick woes.

The Penguins (16-9-4, 36 points) were hardly bothered

by the Islanders, as was evident by a season-best goal output.

Nice way to snap a three-game losing skid, especially with an Atlantic Division showdown at Philadelphia looming Saturday.

Two players scoring hat tricks should settle any doubt that may have crept into an injury-plagued dressing room.

The last Penguins' teammates to tally hat tricks in the same game were Mario Lemieux and Joe Mullen, who pulled it off against the New York Rangers on April 9, 1993.

No sooner had Sykora's hat-trick deflection crossed the goal line than an 80th consecutive sellout crowd at Mellon Arena roared and began tossing hats and promotional giveaway bags onto the ice.

After scoring, Sykora jumped into the arms of Crosby, whom he credited with "calling the play."

"I just told him what I was going to do," said Crosby, who recorded three assists. "We all know the history of (Sykora) and how many games it had been."

That history was reason enough for Dupuis, who ate a post-game shaving-cream facewich from teammate Matt Cooke, to turn praise of his personal-best performance toward Sykora.

However, coach Michel Therrien would have none of it.

"His first goal was a great shot," Therrien said of Dupuis, who opened the scoring with a slap shot blast past New York starting goalie Joey MacDonald at 6:25 of the first period.

Dupuis scored his final two goals, Nos. 5 and 6 of the season, against Dannis, who replaced MacDonald after the first period, which the Penguins ended ahead, 4-1.

"It's got to be good for his confidence," Therrien said of Dupuis' hat trick.

"It's one of those things," Dupuis said. "I felt good shooting, and guys were giving me the puck and finding me.

"But the focus should be on (Sykora)."

The game was one that center Evgeni Malkin said was the "most fun (he's) had in a long time."

Speaking of Malkin, the league's point leader, he was one of several Penguins to pad his stats last night.

Malkin scored his 12th goal and added an assist. He has 48 points through 29 games — 14 better than his total through as many games last season, when he finished second overall in the NHL with 106 points.

Fellow "Mega Powers" center Crosby upped his second-best point total to 44. His only better start through 29 games was 52 points in 2006-07, when he won the scoring title and MVP with a 120-point campaign.

Nine Penguins registered multiple points - including two-point efforts from Cooke, center Jordan Staal, and defensemen Rob Scuderi and Alex Goligoski.

Defenseman Philippe Boucher tallied his first goal as a Penguin after returning from a six-game injury-related absence.

Oh, and right wing Miroslav Satan scored his 11th goal and added two assists last night — matching in the first period his top performance all season. Back to Sykora, who bested MacDonald at 17:40 of the first period. He nailed Danis for the first time at 7:53 of the second.

"When you score that first goal, you start feeling good about yourself — especially when the puck is coming to you," said Sykora, who also added an assist. "And the puck was coming to me."

Greg Shamus/Pittsburgh Penguins

The Penguins **Petr Sykora's** (center) skates back to the bench as hats rain down on the ice.

Joe Sargent/Pittsburgh Penguins

Penguins defenseman **Ryan Whitney** sees his first action of the season against the Tampa Bay Lightning.

TAMPA BAY BLANKS REELING PENGUINS

By Mike Prisuta/TRIB TOTAL MEDIA

○ ○ ○ ○ ○

Wednesday, December 24, 2008

Penguins captain Sidney Crosby has denied the existence of a friendly rivalry with teammate and NHL scoring leader Evgeni Malkin, but Tampa Bay head coach Rick Tocchet has noticed a competition between the two and what it can produce.

"I'm sure there's competitiveness with them against each other, which is great," Tocchet said. "I'm sure both want to make the other guy better.

"I think sometimes you can see that."

Penguins head coach Michel Therrien, meanwhile, has detected no such chemistry or competition of late, and instead found himself bemoaning his team's unwillingness, in his estimation, to pay the price necessary for success.

The depths of Therrien's displeasure will, for the time being, remain a matter of conjecture.

"If I had an hour," he said. "There are a lot of things I don't like, a lot of things."

Tuesday night's 2-0 loss to the Tampa Bay Lightning probably heads the list, with the particulars of what's irking him running close behind.

"We don't have the right attitude," Therrien said. "They like to complain about each other on the bench, on the ice. They better wake up, better wake up pretty quick.

"We're missing players; OK, we're missing players. We've played a lot of games and they're tired. It's really, really disappointing about our work ethic, our concentration. Until we change our attitude, we're going to repeat the same."

The Pens went 0-for-3 on the power play and were outshot, 29-15, while absorbing their first shutout loss of the season.

They fell to 18-12-4 overall and 4-6-0 in their last 10 games after losing for the third time in four tries on home ice.

The Lightning had entered 7-16-9 overall for an NHL-worst 23 points (tied with the New York Islanders).

Tampa Bay had been just 3-13-6 since a three-game winning streak from Oct. 28-Nov. 1, and 2-9-5 since Tocchet replaced Barry Melrose as head coach Nov. 14.

"You lose to the last place team in the league at home and don't get a goal, it doesn't get much worse than that," said Penguins defenseman Ryan Whitney, who made his 2008-09 debut.

Therrien had opened the game skating Evgeni Malkin and Sidney Crosby on a line with Pascal Dupuis.

Malkin and Crosby entered ranked No. 1 and No. 2 in the NHL in scoring (58 points for Malkin, 47 for Crosby).

The pair combined for just three shots (all by Malkin) through the first 40 minutes, after which Tampa Bay had a 1-0 lead and a 22-12 edge in shots.

Therrien separated Malkin and Crosby for the third period, skating Malkin between Ruslan Fedotenko and Petr Sykora and putting Crosby between Dupuis and Miroslav Satan.

The Pens didn't register a shot in the third-period until Malkin was denied on a short-handed breakaway with just over nine minutes left in regulation, seconds before Tampa Bay padded its advantage to 2-0.

"Determination, things like that," Whitney said, when asked what's been wrong of late. "We're losing battles, not getting pucks out (of the defensive zone).

"It's not just a few guys. It's on the whole team."

Whitney returns from lengthy absence

PENS, OILERS TRADE BACKUP GOALIES

By Tricia Lafferty/TRIB TOTAL MEDIA

○ ○ ○ ○ ○

Sunday, January 18, 2009

The Penguins were short a goalie in practice Saturday.

That's because backup goalie Dany Sabourin was packing his bags for Edmonton while newly acquired backup Mathieu Garon was on his way to Pittsburgh.

Sabourin, along with forward Ryan Stone — who played mainly for the Penguins' Wilkes-Barre AHL affiliate — and a fourth-round draft pick in 2011 were traded to the Oilers.

Garon, 31, will become an unrestricted free agent after the season. He did not practice with the Penguins yesterday because he was on a flight from Colorado, where he made 37 saves in a 3-2 win over the Avalanche the night before.

"He's a quality, veteran goaltender," Penguins assistant general manager Chuck Fletcher said. "He has a proven track record in the NHL. He'll add quality depth and bring leadership."

Garon has played in 15 games for Edmonton this season, posting a 6-8-0 record. He owns a 3.17 goals-against

Penguins goaltender **Danny Sabourin** was 6-8-2 in 19 games with the Penguins this season.

average and an .895 save percentage.

"I think it's gonna be a good fit with (starter Marc-Andre) Fleury," Therrien said. "Fleury is still our guy, but we want to make sure he's gonna be well surrounded."

In 19 games with the Penguins this season, Sabourin was 6-8-2 with a .898 save percentage and a 2.85 goals-against average.

TO PLAY, OR NOT TO PLAY?

Center Sidney Crosby practiced yesterday and said it will be a game-time decision whether or not he'll play in today's game against the New York Rangers. He left Wednesday's game with a lower-body injury and did not play Friday night.

"It felt good," Crosby said. "I'm kind of on the fence right now. We'll see with the swelling."

Crosby said he will skate in the pregame warmup to test the injury.

"There were a few things I didn't feel great at (today), but that is a part of injuries," Crosby said. "I still need to make sure I'm comfortable playing a game."

WAITING GAME

Therrien said defensemen Kris Letang (lower body) and Rob Scuderi (head) — who were also injured Wednesday — will be game-time decisions, as well.

Scuderi was hit above the right eye with a wrist shot, which caused bruising and swelling. He was unable to open his eye until Friday morning, but hopes to play today.

"I felt pretty good out there, no effects," he said.

"My vision's good. I can do everything."

AND IN OTHER INJURY NEWS...

Forward Max Talbot was placed on injured reserve retroactive to Wednesday, when he left the game with an upper-body injury. Defenseman Brooks Orpik did not practice yesterday after leaving Friday's game with an undisclosed injury.

Penguins center **Max Talbot** looks to lead the third line this season.

EVGENI MALKIN

MALKIN STEPPING INTO THE LIMELIGHT

By Rob Rossi/TRIB TOTAL MEDIA

○ ○ ○ ○ ○

Sunday, February 15, 2009

The size 11.5 boots belong to a reserved 22-year-old who has produced more points than any NHL player over the past two seasons, a gentle giant one teammate labeled "a complete clown" for his behind-closed-doors behavior and the man a former league MVP and scoring champion identified as "the most talented player in the world."

Those are some big skates Penguins center Evgeni "Geno" Malkin has to fill.

Of course, nothing about Malkin's transformation from hockey's best and quietest rookie in 2006 to one of its most talked-about, if not talkative, players today has proven easy.

"He just makes it look that way," Penguins defenseman Brooks Orpik said. "It's easy to watch what he's doing this year, last year and since he came here and forget that he left everything he knew three years ago — his entire world in Russia, his family, friends and life — to play in North America, where the game is played on a smaller rink. It's a different style, really.

"All that, and he's one of the best players on the planet every night. I don't think people mention that enough. I get the feeling a lot of people take for granted how tough it was and probably is at times still for him. The people that know Geno best know what he's gone through to get where he is right now."

Right now, Malkin is the NHL scoring leader, a Penguins leader as alternate captain and, according to San Jose Sharks center Joe Thornton, "probably the best player in the world."

"He can do it all," said Thornton, the 2006 MVP and scoring champion. "He can shoot as well as anybody. He can pass as well as anybody. He makes big plays when his team needs it. He uses his size to his advantage, and he's such a strong skater, with that next-gear burst.

"When you have that size and that skill — hey, Malkin's the most talented player in the world. I think he's also the best."

MAGNIFICENT, THEY DARE SAY

○ ○ ○ ○ ○

Malkin's skill is a marvel to teammates and opponents.

At 6-foot-3, 195 pounds, he is a tall pivot with a lanky frame that he uses to shield the puck from opposing players.

"He's kind of a physical freak," Penguins center Jordan Staal said. "You can't get the puck off him when he really wants to keep it. I've seen a lot of guys try, and they've all failed."

Blessed with deceptive speed, a hard and accurate shot, hawk-like vision, inherent awareness and a game-changing flair — he recently scored twice and set up a goal in the third period of a 4-3 overtime home win

EVGENI MALKIN

against Tampa Bay — Malkin has drawn a particular comparison that no player would invite.

No player that wears a skating penguin crest, anyway.

"Maybe," Phoenix coach Wayne Gretzky said of Malkin, "he's a little bit like Mario."

No faint praise, considering it comes from the NHL's all-time leading scorer and refers to a fellow Hall of Famer, current Penguins majority co-owner Mario Lemieux.

Even the most conservative evaluations of Malkin, who had averaged a league-best 1.35 points in his past 138 games prior to Saturday, turn effusive after a few seconds.

"He's definitely one of the best five forwards in the league, no question," Ottawa captain Daniel Alfredsson said, adding that Malkin stands out because of his physicality.

"He's so strong on his skates. He can beat you one-on-one. He's not just a goal-scorer. He's a shooter and a passer, and he's really good at drawing attention and finding the open guy."

Malkin's teammates, including 2007 MVP and scoring champion Sidney Crosby, do not dispute these assessments. Of course, what the Penguins like best about Malkin is the stuff most people miss because, as center Max Talbot noted, "people tend to treat him differently."

"Only the (Pittsburgh) media talks to him, mostly, and a lot of fans — look, they love Geno, they go crazy for him, but he doesn't get approached like you might think. It's like people have heard or read he doesn't speak English, so his personality isn't really out there because nobody outside of our team has taken time to know what he's really like."

AN UNSPOKEN ARRANGEMENT

Crosby has spent much of the season as the NHL's second-leading scorer and the majority of his career as the face of the league. The Nova Scotia native speaks more French, his second language, before one game in Montreal than Malkin talks English, his second language, over a week in Pittsburgh.

Malkin did not agree to his first English-only interview with local media until early last season. He still is rarely pressed to answer questions following Penguins' practices and games — and he admitted that "talking every day" isn't high on his priority list, hence his occasional quick escapes or ducks into the medical room.

"I'd just rather play hockey," Malkin said. "I look at Sid after practice — and it's a lot. I don't know how he can play the game like he does after doing all that. It's amazing. He does so much. Because of Sid, I can just play. That's good for me."

Crosby, who has placed phone calls to reporters upon requests through the Penguins' media relations staff, does not believe Malkin deserves criticism for occasional reluctance to answer questions in a foreign language.

Crosby admitted he was amused upon first hearing of speculation that he and Malkin had an arrangement in which Crosby would handle media responsibilities to afford Malkin time to concentrate on hockey.

"If we have an arrangement, it's to do what's in the best interest of this team," Crosby said. "For me and Geno, it's to make sure we help each other be better.

"That (media) stuff comes with being comfortable, and it will for Geno. Maybe he's not completely there with the media, but I can honestly say he's become one of the guys around us — and that's been fun to see, really fun.

"When he wasn't speaking as much, it was kind of hard to understand what kind of guy he was. We've had three years to get to know him, and what we've all learned is that he's an easy-going guy."

Malkin also has shown a comical side.

The day before the Penguins faced Detroit at home in an anticipated rematch of the Stanley Cup Final, Malkin was among a group of teammates first off the ice after practice. When the dressing room opened to the media, Malkin, smiling all the while, waved reporters and cameramen toward teammate Matt Cooke.

"Detroit is easy," Malkin said in a sarcastic tone. "Cookie will get a hat trick."

Cooke, an agitator, not a goal-scorer, rolled his eyes.

Malkin did likewise before adding: "Matt Cooke, hat trick, write it down ...

"Bye everybody."

FOR RUSSIA, WITH LOVE

Orpik, one of Malkin's earliest and closest friends among the Penguins, described him as "a proud guy who cares more than anybody knows."

A list of what Malkin said he cares about: winning the Stanley Cup ("my dream"); family ("wonderful"); teammates ("great guys"); his new suburban Pittsburgh house ("nice, sometimes dirty"); post-game massages ("they really help"); and his mother's borscht ("so good").

He said money — he signed a five-year extension worth $43.5 million in July — is of no concern. He also will not lose a minute of sleep if he fails to hold off Crosby or Washington forward Alex Ovechkin for the Art Ross Trophy as the league's leading scorer.

"I don't think about it," Malkin said. "Nobody believes me, though."

On the subject of Ovechkin, his Russian rival and the only player selected ahead of Malkin in the 2004 entry draft: Their two-year feud, which during Penguins-Capitals games turned nasty, was laid to rest last month in Montreal at the All-Star Game.

Their sudden shift from foes to friends occurred for one reason.

"Russia, all of that for Russia," Malkin said, acknowledging that a fellow countryman, Atlanta captain Ilya Kovalchuk, spoke to him and Ovechkin and urged them to reconcile for the benefit of Russia's chance for gold at the 2010 Winter Olympics in Vancouver.

"We went to dinner and had a good talk," Malkin said. "(Kovalchuk) is a good guy. He said, 'You guys (were) friends, be friends again for Russia.' After that, it was all good."

Kovalchuk — who said the confidence Malkin has gained from NHL success should give the Russian hockey team an advantage in Vancouver — is not surprised that Malkin put aside personal differences with Ovechkin in the name of patriotism.

"He's proud to be Russian and proud to be on the national team," Kovalchuk said. "It's everything. It's a huge honor. Hockey is everything in Russia."

RESISTING TRANSFORMATION

○○○○○

His Russian heritage is important to Malkin. He spends summers in Moscow and St. Petersburg, hoping to soak up as much of those cities' histories as he can before training sessions, which begin in early July.

Malkin carries two cell phones, one for texting in Russian. The movies he watches he first views versions with Russian overdubs.

"When we ordered movies on the road, he'd only let me order ones he had seen already — the Russian versions," Talbot said. "I think that is how he started to learn English, by watching two versions of every movie that came out, like 'Transformers.'"

Orpik said Malkin has denied taking English lessons last summer, but suspects he did so begrudgingly.

"Like a lot of Russian players, he's proud of where he comes from and himself for coming this far," Orpik said. "It's just the type of people they are. They have a tremendous sense of self pride, and Geno isn't any different.

"It's not an easy situation for him to work here, spend most of the year here and get about two months in Russia to reconnect with everything. It's almost like there is going to be two sides of him for as long as he's playing in the NHL.

"The thing is, there's a great hockey player no matter what side you see."

MALKIN ON MALKIN

○○○○○

Penguins star Evgeni Malkin granted the Trib Total Media an exclusive 15-minute interview in English on Tuesday. Here is an excerpt:

TTM: How are you different today than when you arrived in Pittsburgh in 2006 as a 20-year-old from Russia?

EM: It's not too much different. I feel comfortable now in my career. My English is a little bit better. Everything is going good.

Now I understand how to play in the NHL. The first year was hard. The second was only good. Now, it's a little bit easy — the hockey. (Laughs) Maybe I shouldn't say that.

TTM: The North American hockey media often refers to you as "shy" and "uncomfortable." Does that bother you?

EM: I don't care if people think that way. I care what my teammates (think). I care about playing hockey, helping the Penguins win.

TTM: Do you wish people would speak to you more often in English, maybe get to know you better?

EM: Yeah. (Laughs) But not like with Sid.

The Penguins' **Evgeni Malkin** wears a shirt dedicated to the fallen Pittsburgh police officers as he gives his game jersey away.

PENGUINS PART WAYS WITH COACH THERRIEN

By Rob Rossi and Mike Prisuta/TRIB TOTAL MEDIA

○ ○ ○ ○ ○

Monday, February 16, 2009

Players were as surprised as anybody that Michel Therrien was relieved of his coaching duties by the Penguins late Sunday.

"We were shocked," goalie Marc-Andre Fleury said from a hotel in the New York area; the Penguins will face the Islanders at 2 p.m. at Nassau Coliseum.

"The mood at practice was pretty down (following a 6-2 loss at Toronto on Saturday), but nobody thought this was coming. We had our usual meetings about that game. Really, nobody that I talked to expected this."

Therrien, who did not return phone calls, was replaced on an interim basis by Dan Bylsma, who was in his first season as a professional head coach with Wilkes-Barre of the AHL.

Five games shy of surpassing Ed Johnston's franchise-best 276 consecutive games as Penguins coach, Therrien took the fall for an underachieving club. The Penguins (27-25-5, 59 points) were 10th in the Eastern Conference as of yesterday, five points out of the eighth and final playoff spot.

General manager Ray Shero said everybody associated with the Penguins is accountable for the club's struggles after a 12-4-3 start.

Their 15-21-2 record since Nov. 22 — not the loss Saturday at Toronto, in which the Penguins blew a 2-0 lead to finish the season series 1-3-0 against the lowly Maple Leafs — convinced Shero that firing Therrien was his only option.

"I didn't particularly like the direction the team was headed (in)," Shero said. "I've watched for a number of weeks. I didn't feel comfortable."

Therrien was the only coach Shero had known since replacing former general manager Craig Patrick on May 25, 2006. He also was one of the most successful bench bosses in team history, with a 135-105-32 overall record after replacing Eddie Olczyk on Dec. 15, 2005.

A Jack Adams Award finalist as the NHL's top coach for the 2006-07 season, his first full season with the Penguins, Therrien returned playoff hockey to Pittsburgh after a seven-year absence with a 47-point turnaround — the fourth-best single-season improvement in NHL history.

Under Therrien, Sidney Crosby transformed from a heralded rookie to the youngest captain in league history at 20 prior to last season. The Penguins also made the playoffs twice, going 15-10 and coming within two wins of the Stanley Cup last season, losing a six-game final to Detroit.

Shero signed Therrien to a three-year contract this past summer, agreeing to pay him around $1 million annually.

In an interview with Trib Total Media last month, Shero said Therrien deserved the chance to get the Penguins through "tough times."

"Every time we've gone through it, we've found our way through," Shero said Jan. 22. "That's what I go on. That's what I know. I've got to give the coaching staff some credit. They've found a way the past couple of years.

"I believe we're in the process of finding a way through some tough times again."

The Penguins went 4-4-1 after Shero's quasi-vote of confidence.

Players know this move was made with one objective.

"We were told to try and rediscover the fun and enjoy the game," forward Miroslav Satan said of the message Bylsma delivered at a 10 p.m. meeting last night. "Time will tell if this move works. It's up to us. We all know missing the playoffs is not an option, but I believe we have the team to make the playoffs.

"We can be a great team."

Right wing Petr Sykora said the Penguins have seemed "a little step behind" all season.

"It kind of feels like the team hasn't had the same fire that we did last year," Sykora said. "We're all kind of searching for answers."

Sykora said Therrien's firing is an indication that either those answers will be found, or ...

"Nobody should be surprised if something else happens," he said. "It's all about winning in this league. I wouldn't be surprised at anything. Management is going to do what's best for this team to be successful — and successful for us is the playoffs."

The Penguins are engaged in trade talks with several teams. The trade deadline is March 4.

Bylsma, who was 35-16-1-2 with the AHL Penguins this season, was hired by Shero as an AHL assistant for the 2006-07 season.

He knows many of the players he will coach, and he knows what he wants to see from them.

"I want other teams to deal with our speed and skill," said Bylsma, whom Shero called an "up-and-coming coach in the game."

Assistant Mike Yeo and goalie coach Gilles Meloche were retained by the Penguins to work with Bylsma. Andre Savard, an assistant who worked with the defense, was re-assigned to an unspecified role in the organization.

Director of player personnel Tom Fitzgerald will join Bylsma's staff as an assistant.

THERRIEN'S TIME

Penguins regular-season coaching record: 135-105-32

Penguins postseason coaching record: 15-10

Career highlights

Dec. 15, 2005 — Therrien replaces Eddie Olczyk as coach. Under his guidance, the Penguins go 14-29-8, but finish the season 22-46-14 overall and last in the Eastern Conference.

Dec. 29, 2006 — Penguins begin a 14-0-2 streak that propels them into the Stanley Cup playoffs for the first time since the 2000-01 season.

April 19, 2007 — Penguins lose their opening round Stanley Cup playoff series to Ottawa, 4-1.

April 6, 2008 — Therrien leads the Penguins to a 47-27-8 regular-season record and their first Atlantic Division title. It was the team's first division title of any kind since winning the Northeast Division under Kevin Constantine in the 1997-98 season.

June 4, 2008 — Penguins lose the Stanley Cup Finals, 4-2, to the Detroit Red Wings.

July 18, 2008 — The Penguins and GM Ray Shero announce they agree to a three-year contract extension with Therrien to keep him as coach through the 2010-11 season at a salary approaching $1 million annually.

Feb. 15, 2009 — After a 27-25-5 start to the 2008-09 season, Therrien is fired and replaced on an interim basis by Dan Bylsma.

Former Penguins coach **Michel Therrien** on the bench at Mellon Arena.

Chaz Palla/Trib Total Media

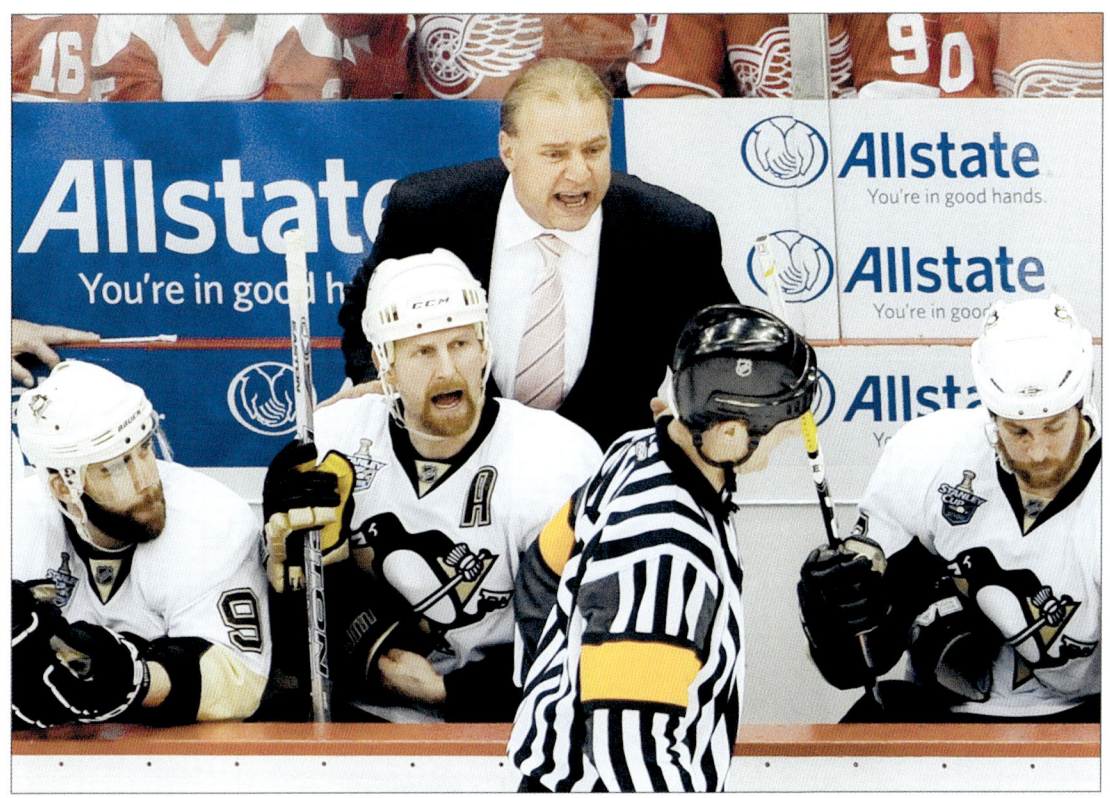

Chaz Palla/Trib Total Media

Former Penguins coach **Michel Therrien** voices his displeasure with a referee during the Stanley Cup Final in 2008.

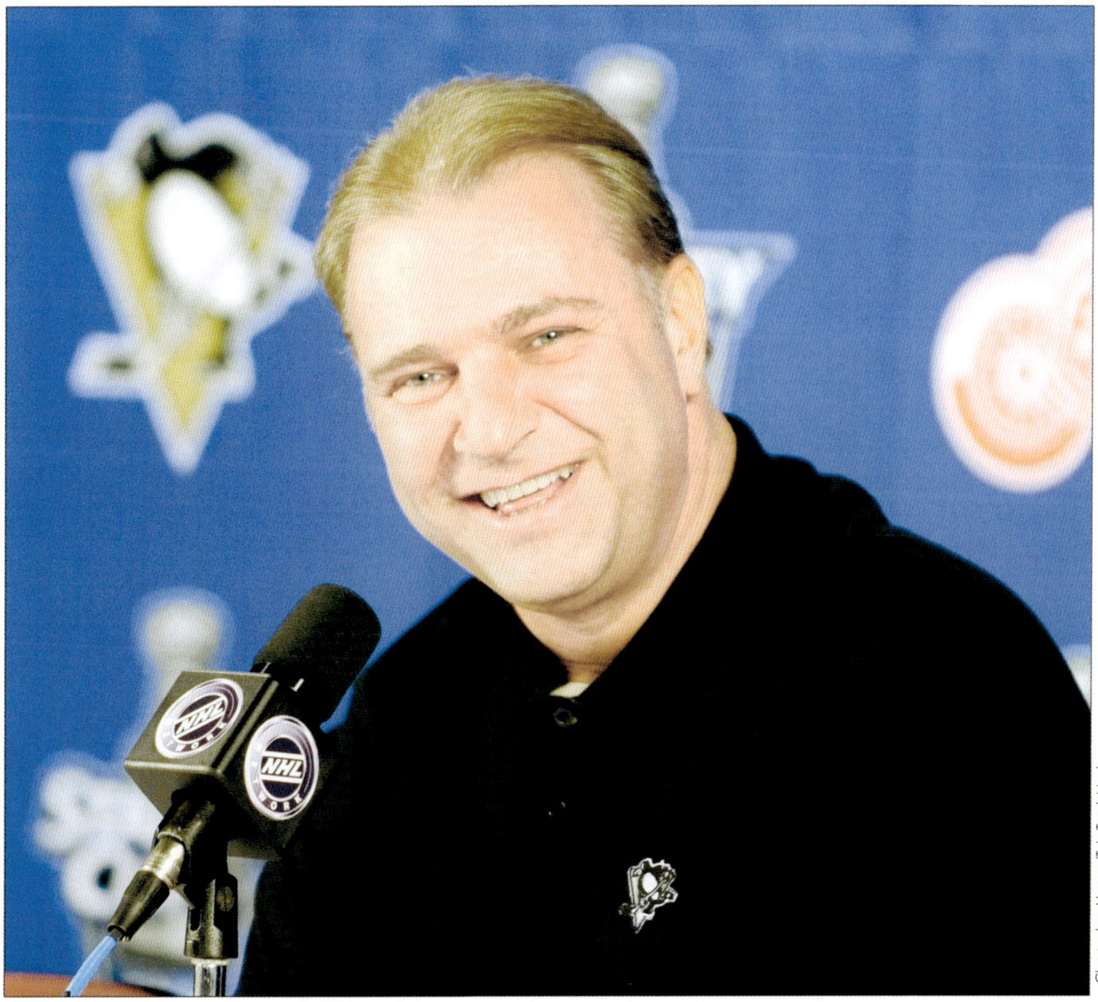

Christopher Horner/Trib Total Media

Former Penguins coach **Michel Therrien** shares a lighter moment during a 2008 Stanley Cup Final press conference.

Penguins defenseman **Sergei Gonchar** celebrates his game-winning goal with teammate **Pascal Dupuis**.

LEADERS FUEL PENGUINS' THIRD-PERIOD SURGE

By Rob Rossi/TRIB TOTAL MEDIA

○ ○ ○ ○ ○

Friday, February 20, 2009

Theirs is an advantage few hockey teams of this or any era can match, especially if the score is tied entering the third period, as was the scenario Thursday night.

However, after he scored the Penguins' first of three third-period goals in a 5-4 victory against the Montreal Canadiens at Mellon Arena, center Evgeni Malkin sheepishly said "no" when asked if his club benefitted from employing him and fellow "Mega Power" Sidney Crosby, third among league point producers.

"Apparently that's why Geno's a player and not a coach," interim coach Dan Bylsma said of Malkin, who leads the NHL with 84 points after a two-point performance last night.

Players such as Malkin, Crosby and defenseman Sergei Gonchar — remember him? — provided the leadership-by-example last night that Bylsma said earlier in the day he wanted to see.

Malkin scored his team-leading 26th goal 29 seconds into the third period to break a 2-2 tie, besting Montreal goalie Carey Price with a crisp shot after receiving a sharp pass from Crosby.

Gonchar delivered a sweet "thanks" to local fans who supported him through five months of recovery from left shoulder surgery with his first goal of the season at 7:18 — a vintage slap shot that eluded Price to provide the Penguins a lead they would not surrender.

Wingers Petr Sykora and Miroslav Satan scored their 22nd and 15th goals, respectively, and forward Max Talbot added his seventh tally and first in nine games to give the Penguins (28-25-6, 62 points) a crucial — or, as Talbot said, "must-have" — victory.

"It was obviously a game we needed to win," Talbot said of the Penguins, who remain 10th in the Eastern Conference, but now only four points behind eighth-place Buffalo, which lost at Philadelphia.

Florida, which lost at Chicago, remains seventh with 66 points and ninth-place Carolina, a winner at the New York Islanders, owns 63 points.

As for the Canadiens, 3-11-1 since Jan. 20, their grip on a playoff spot is weakening. This loss leaves them with 67 points — only four more than the Hurricanes and five up on the Penguins, who snapped a two-game losing streak that followed a 3-1-0 home stand.

"This is our playoffs," Crosby said.

To reach the postseason, the Penguins will need to fully master the commands of Bylsma, who has preached "aggressiveness" since replacing Michel Therrien on Sunday.

Bylsma, who was promoted to the NHL in his first full professional season as head coach with AHL affiliate Wilkes-Barre/Scranton, said he "saw good things" from the Penguins last night.

"Going into the offensive zone with speed, especially," Bylsma said. "And we got to play defense a little quicker.

"They had a clear understanding of how we want to play, but it wasn't perfect."

Good enough, though, the Penguins will take it. Malkin and Crosby have been more than that all season, and Talbot figures that will continue over the final 23 games.

"We have the two best players in the league right now," Talbot said. "They can be magic."

PENS SHIP WHITNEY TO ANAHEIM FOR WINGER

By Tricia Lafferty/TRIB TOTAL MEDIA

Friday, February 27, 2009

Ryan Whitney was labeled one of the Penguins' 'core players' after signing a six-year contract extension in July 2007.

For the second time in a little more than three months, Penguins general manager Ray Shero determined the best way to improve his team was by trading a popular defenseman.

On Nov. 16, the guy to go was Darryl Sydor — shipped to Dallas for another defenseman, Philippe Boucher.

Thursday morning, the Penguins dealt defenseman Ryan Whitney, once labeled by Shero as part of the franchise "core," to the Anaheim Ducks for gritty winger Chris Kunitz and prized prospect Eric Tangradi.

A lot of factors played into Shero's willingness to part with Whitney, a skilled offensive defenseman who in July 2007 was the first so-called "core player" he signed to a lengthy extension — six years, $24 million.

The biggest factors, though, were depth at offensive-minded defensemen and a dire need for an improved winger to play on one of the Penguins' two top scoring lines.

"With the emergence of Kris Letang and with (Sergei) Gonchar coming back and with Alex Goligoski and his development this year, it gave us one extra defenseman to try to get a top-six forward like we have with Chris Kunitz," Shero said.

Kunitz, 29, scored 16 goals and recorded 19 assists to go with 55 penalty minutes in 62 games this season with the Ducks. He was part of their 2007 Stanley Cup winning team and this season was their leader with 148 hits.

He is signed through 2011-12 at an annual cap hit of $3,725,000 — just $275,000 less than Whitney.

Kunitz is expected to play tonight at Chicago.

"It kind of came out of the blue, but when I sat down and thought about it, it's a great move for my career," said Kunitz, adding that he looked forward to playing with Sidney Crosby and Evgeni Malkin.

"The Penguins are only a couple of points out, and this is a (five-game) road trip. It's important for me to help us get points right away."

Whitney, 26, was not with the Penguins yesterday. He left the team Wednesday to be with his mother, Sue, who underwent successful brain surgery.

He received good news on that front — and perhaps word of long-term benefit on a professional level.

Anaheim general manager Bob Murray coveted a puck-moving defenseman to grow with a young nucleus that includes center Ryan Getzlaf and wingers Corey Perry and Bobby Ryan.

"I'm a big believer in building from the back end, and our back end wasn't good enough," said Murray, who may deal either Scott Neidermayer or Chris Pronger before the March 4 trade deadline.

Though popular among teammates for his good-natured demeanor, Whitney came to expect a trade over the past few months — especially with a logjam at defense and the cost certainty of his contract.

"I'm a little surprised, yeah, but with the team they have there and the guys they have coming up, it's not too surprising when I think about it," said Whitney, who planned to play for the Ducks last night at Boston before they traveled to Dallas for a game against the Stars.

Whitney played in only 28 games for the Penguins this season, missing much of the first half after left foot surgery in August. He scored two goals and recorded 11 assists and was a minus-15 — statistics that back up his assessment that he "hasn't played the way (he's) capable."

That undeniable fact also made him a luxury the Penguins, on the outside of the Eastern playoff bubble, could not afford.

"They have two young (defensemen) in Alex and Kris who are good players, make less money than me and are younger than me." Letang, 21, counts $835,000 against the cap and will be a restricted free agent after next season. Goligoski, 22, counts $984,000 against the cap and can become a restricted free agent July 1.

As restricted free agents, the Penguins own both players' rights.

Shero and Penguins interim coach Dan Bylsma described Kunitz as a gritty player who creates space and spends a lot of time around the net. Bylsma played with and coached Kunitz.

"He's going to go to the net, going to get to the puck first, and he's going be a guy that (hits)," Bylsma said. "That's what we're going to demand, and I'm sure Chris is going be ready to do that."

Bylsma added that Kunitz was "an ingredient we needed to add to the lineup."

Shero would not say if he was done dealing before the deadline.

"We'll see," Shero said. "This is the first step, and we'll see where we go."

Tangradi, 20, likely will take some time to develop. A Philadelphia native, he is in his third season with the Belleville Bulls of the Ontario Hockey League, where he ranks second with 87 points (38 goals, 49 assists).

"He's really raw," Shero said. "He's got big-time physical ability — good hands and hockey sense."

MALKIN LIFTS PENGUINS IN OVERTIME THRILLER

By Rob Rossi/TRIB TOTAL MEDIA

Saturday, February 27, 2009

Newly acquired winger **Chris Kunitz** returns to the bench after scoring his first goal as a Penguin.

CHICAGO — The opponent had one of hockey's promising young stars stringing together a strong performance.

The Penguins had Evgeni Malkin, hockey's best young player, doing what an MVP candidate does, scoring in overtime to deliver an extra, must-have point to his desperate club.

Malkin scored a power-play goal at 1:36 of the extra period — his 28th tally to pad his league-leading point total to 89. The Penguins overcame a pair of blown two-goal leads and young Chicago captain Jonathan Toews' first hat trick in a 5-4 victory Friday over the Blackhawks at United Center.

"Those points, we need them so bad right now," said defenseman Sergei Gonchar, who recorded one of his two assists on Malkin's winner. "We're battling and fighting, and we needed this."

The Penguins (31-26-6, 68 points) moved within a point of idle Buffalo for the eighth and final Eastern Conference playoff spot. Fifth-place Montreal won last night at Philadelphia to build a five-point lead on the Penguins, who are on a 7-3-1 stretch.

Buffalo and ninth-place Carolina (each with 69 points), the seventh-place New York Rangers and sixth-place Florida (both at 70) all play tonight. The Penguins, outside the playoff bubble, play Sunday at Dallas — the second of a critical five-game road trip.

Malkin stole the spotlight from Toews, whose power-play goals late in the first period and early in the second rallied the Blackhawks from a 2-0 deficit. The Penguins had gone ahead, 2-0, in the first period on goals by center Jordan Staal, his 16th and first in 14 games, and recently acquired left wing Chris Kunitz, his 17th and first in his Pittsburgh debut.

Chicago's Toews was originally awarded a third power-play goal at 15:09 of the second period, giving the Blackhawks a 3-2 lead. However, replay officials ruled he deflected a puck past Penguins goalie Marc-Andre Fleury with a high stick and disallowed it.

Given new life after the reversal, the Penguins scored twice in the final three minutes of the second. Winger Miroslav Satan netted his 16th at 18:24, forward Max Talbot his ninth at 19:01, and the Penguins carried a two-goal lead into the third-period intermission.

Even at that point, two points for a win that Talbot would call "huge," seemed no sure thing for the Penguins.

Satan was penalized for tripping 31 seconds into the third period, giving the Blackhawks' power-play another chance to do damage.

Toews' 25th goal — and, finally, that first hat trick — came at 1:55 of the third period. It was another power-play goal, and it pulled the Blackhawks to within one goal, 4-3.

Chicago pulled even at 4-4 on center David Bolland's 14th goal at 15:15. The Blackhawks outshot the Penguins, 20-4, over the final 20 minutes.

"We knew we needed the (extra) point," said the Penguins' Fleury, who made 41 saves. "We've been playing better lately, and we believe more in ourselves; we've not been getting down when things go bad, so we were still confident we could get the extra point."

Confidence is a luxury for any team that possesses a talent such as Malkin.

Of course, as Gonchar noted, "not many teams do."

The Penguins actually have two such all-everything young stars: Malkin, 22, and 21-year-old captain and league No. 3 scorer Sidney Crosby, who missed a second consecutive game due to a sore groin.

"Those guys, they have special things inside of them," Gonchar said. "This time it was 'Geno' that gave us the game-winner.

"To be honest, we could have played a lot better in the third. But you know, with the position we are in, I'll take it."

GM SHERO ADDS MORE GRIT AT NHL DEADLINE

By Rob Rossi/TRIB TOTAL MEDIA

Thursday, March 5, 2009

General manager Ray Shero believes he has made the Penguins tougher over the past week by adding hard-edged forwards Chris Kunitz, Bill Guerin and Craig Adams.

Each of those players — Guerin and Adams acquired Wednesday prior to the 3 p.m. NHL trade deadline — has won the Stanley Cup.

Shero is not sure they are the missing pieces to a repeat Cup run for the defending Eastern Conference champion Penguins, but he does think his club is "solidified" as a playoff team.

Given their standing Feb. 15, when interim coach Dan Bylsma replaced Michel Therrien, the Penguins will take that — and take their chances if they reach the postseason.

"We've put together a little streak here and certainly have a long way to go, and we're going to need help from everybody, including our newcomers," Shero said yesterday of the Penguins (33-26-6, 72 points), who are 6-1-1 with Bylsma.

The help Shero handed Bylsma yesterday will be in the lineup tonight at Florida against the Panthers (33-23-3, 74 points).

Prior to the deadline, the Penguins held the eighth and final Eastern Conference playoff spot.

They are 3-0-0 since Shero's pre-deadline-day strike last Thursday, when he sent defenseman Ryan Whitney to Anaheim for Kunitz and prospect Eric Tangradi.

Kunitz, repeatedly described as a "top six winger" by Penguins brass, has scored three goals and recorded five points in three games with the Penguins.

Guerin, acquired yesterday from the New York Islanders in exchange for a conditional pick in the June entry draft, would not guarantee a similar start. However, he said his style at age 38 has not changed from when he broke into the league at 21 in 1991.

"I'm the same player I've always been: I go to the net; I like to shoot the puck; I try to bring a physical presence; and I try to be a good teammate — those are the important things," said Guerin, who like Adams can become an unrestricted free agent July 1.

The Islanders' captain and "a great leader," according to New York general manager Garth Snow, Guerin waived a no-movement clause to join the Penguins. He is a right-handed shot and should get a crack at playing with Kunitz and center Sidney Crosby, who has missed four consecutive games with a sore groin.

Shero said Bylsma will make lineup decisions but said Guerin "can still play with good players."

The Penguins' two top players are centers Evgeni Malkin, the NHL scoring leader, and Crosby, who ranks third.

Guerin (16 goals in 61 games) will cost the Penguins at least their fifth-round pick at the draft, a fourth-round pick if they reach the playoffs and a third-round pick if they advance past the opening round. That third-round pick is not the one Shero acquired from Tampa Bay last June for the rights to wingers Ryan Malone and Gary Roberts.

The offseason losses of Malone, Roberts and wingers Jarkko Ruutu and Adam Hall made these Penguins far too easy to play against, Shero said yesterday.

Snagging Kunitz, Guerin and Adams — a checking-line forward claimed yesterday off waivers from Chicago — addresses a need for "some jam," Shero said.

The moves yesterday also made winger Miroslav Satan expendable.

Satan cleared waivers at noon and was assigned to Wilkes-Barre of the AHL — a procedural move that allows the Penguins to remove his remaining salary from the salary cap.

Within about $1.5 million of the $56.7 million cap after acquiring Kunitz, the Penguins have no space to keep Satan, Guerin and Adams, 31.

Satan, 34, scored 17 goals in 65 games with the Penguins. He signed a one-year contract worth $3.5 million in July — presumably to play with Crosby, though he spent most of the past four months on a checking line.

"We had a harder time getting him on the top two lines, even with (Bylsma) coming in — and he had a good relationship with (Satan)," Shero said. "He's been almost a rover ... he's kind of moved around.

"He's not a fourth-line guy. He needs to play higher. Picking up Kunitz and Guerin, that makes it difficult here."

Newcomers **Bill Guerin** and **Chris Kunitz** immediately became Sidney Crosby's wingers upon their arrivals to Pittsburgh.

Christopher Horner/Trib Total Media

NEW PENGUINS

Bill Guerin
Age: 38
Born: Wilbraham, Mass.
College: Boston College, 2 years
Height: 6-2
Weight: 220
Position: RW
Shoots: Right

Career highlights: Drafted in 1989 in the first round (fifth overall) by the New Jersey Devils. ... Penguins are his eighth NHL team, following Dallas Stars, Boston Bruins, Edmonton Oilers, St. Louis Blues, San Jose Sharks, Devils and New York Islanders. ... Won a Stanley Cup with Devils in 1995, the World Cup in 1996 and a silver medal for the United States in the 2002 Olympics. ... Scored career-high 41 goals with Bruins in 2001-02. ... Had career-high 69 points with Stars in 2003-04.

Trib take: He won't score much more than re-assigned RW Miroslav Satan, but Guerin will make his presence felt in the corners and inside the dressing room.

Craig Adams
Age: 31
Born: Seria, Brunei
College: Harvard, 1 year
Height: 6-0
Weight: 200
Position: RW
Shoots: Right

Career highlights: Although born overseas, grew up in Calgary, where he learned to play hockey. ... Was the last player drafted by the Hartford Whalers, going in the ninth round of the 1996 draft. ... Made his debut in 2000-01 with the relocated Carolina Hurricanes. ... Set career highs in goals (10) and points (21) with the Hurricanes in 2005-06 when they won the Stanley Cup. ... Was traded to the Blackhawks on Jan. 17, 2008.

Trib take: He'll do anything interim coach Dan Bylsma asks, giving the Penguins another rugged fourth-line presence to go with RW Eric Godard.

Penguins captain **Sidney Crosby** scored a second-period goal to ignite his team.

PENGUINS KEEP ROLLING THROUGH OPPONENTS

By Tricia Lafferty/TRIB TOTAL MEDIA

○ ○ ○ ○ ○

Sunday, March 6, 2009

SUNRISE, Fla. — Winning four consecutive games was impressive for the once struggling Penguins, but the fifth victory, perhaps, was the most convincing.

The Penguins made a strong case in their 4-1 win against Florida on Thursday night at BankAtlantic Center that they're serious about making a run not only to the playoffs, but maybe through them.

Just three weeks ago, the Penguins seemed to be fighting for their playoff lives, but now, under interim coach Dan Bylsma, they are sitting alongside sixth-place Florida, which has played one less game than the Penguins.

"It was a benchmark game," defenseman Mark Eaton said. "We played some good hockey leading up to here but hadn't really put a complete game together, and we did that (last night). I think since Dan has taken over, it's been by far our best and most complete game."

Despite falling behind, 1-0, the Penguins scored four unanswered goals, including two from forward Tyler Kennedy.

A red-hot Marc-Andre Fleury made 31 saves to lead the Penguins to their fourth consecutive win on this five-game road trip.

The Penguins — without top defenseman Sergei Gonchar, who was in Pittsburgh with his wife for the birth of their second child — haven't yet exceeded the expectations of their coach, despite their 7-1-1 showing since he took over for Michel Therrien.

"We can't win all five (games) of the trip if we didn't get this one," Bylsma said. "The guys played a great game, probably our best game on the trip for 60 minutes. We spent a lot of time in the offensive zone."

The 47 shots the Penguins fired were proof of that, and Sidney Crosby's goal ignited the Penguins' offensive spark.

Just 24 seconds after Radek Dvorak gave the Panthers a 1-0 lead 2:11 into the second period, Crosby responded.

Crosby — in his first game back since missing four games with a sore groin — maneuvered his way through two Florida defenders before scoring a momentum-stealing goal.

"That's a huge answer," Bylsma said. "We played a pretty good game up till that point. They got the first goal, and it could have been a deflator. But the captain answered right back with a great goal. The telephone was ringing; that was a big answer."

Kennedy gave the Penguins their first lead with his third-period goal, and defenseman Kris Letang extended the advantage to 3-1 just 2:13 later. Kennedy scored again to secure the victory.

"I think it shows we have a lot of depth," Kennedy said of his two-goal night. "I think we have four lines that can all contribute, and that's hard to play against.

Bylsma said Wednesday that "three games against these guys should be a telltale sign of how things could end up for us."

If last night was any indication, the Penguins could be in good shape by the time the regular season ends.

The two teams will meet again Tuesday at Mellon Arena in another crucial game and will close the season series April 5 in Florida.

Things will only heat up for these two teams, as they lobby for playoff positions.

The Penguins and the Panthers, who previously won three of four, all on the road, played an even first period before the scoring started in the second.

The Penguins' offense — with the recently acquired Chris Kunitz, Craig Adams and Bill Guerin — started jelling in the second period and outshot the Panthers, 19-10.

"They fit right in," Bylsma said of the newest Penguins. "They were on the same page immediately."

Crosby returns from four-game absence

SIDNEY CROSBY

PRESSURE CONTINUES TO PURSUE CROSBY

By Rob Rossi/TRIB TOTAL MEDIA

○ ○ ○ ○ ○

Sunday, March 8, 2009

So far, Penguins captain Sidney Crosby's season hasn't gone as planned — verbal jabs from opponents, public denouncements from the media and criticism from fans.

Plus, his club, two victories shy of the Stanley Cup last year, is currently fighting for a playoff spot.

Perhaps those are the reasons Crosby, the player often called "the Face of the NHL," has smiled a lot less this season.

"It's probably always something you deal with when a team is not doing as well," Crosby said of the vitriol aimed at him in recent months. "They look at leadership."

The hockey world has looked at Crosby, who turned 21 only seven months ago, as a savior for so long that some National Hockey League players wonder if he has become a victim of unrealistic expectations.

"I can only imagine how he feels and what he goes through," longtime Dallas Stars center Mike Modano said. "He's the guy who is supposed to carry this league for the next 15 years. That must feel like the weight of the world on his shoulders.

"And it's not just in Pittsburgh, he feels it everywhere."

Those closest to Crosby have noticed.

"Everyone expects so much out of him," said former Penguins winger Ryan Malone, who spent three seasons occupying the locker next to Crosby before his trade to Tampa Bay last June. "For whatever reason, this year people are really kind of all over him."

"Crosby got too much hype than what he truly is — not the best player in the world by a long shot."
— Penguins fan Pat Schrecengost of Kittanning

Over the past four months, Crosby and rival Alexander Ovechkin, 23, of the Washington Capitals — the player who bested him for top rookie honors in 2006 and the guy who last season supplanted him as leading scorer and MVP — have taken turns holding the second spot in the points race.

Penguins center Evgeni Malkin, 22, has topped the scoring list since November.

San Jose center Joe Thornton, a former MVP and scoring champion, said last month Malkin was "the best player in the world."

During an NBC broadcast of the Penguins-Capitals game Feb. 22, analyst and former league general manager Mike Milbury described Ovechkin as "the best player in the world, by far."

That title once belonged to Crosby, who is in the first season of a five-year contract that totals $43.5 million.

SIDNEY CROSBY

He was the first Canadian prospect charged with "saving the game," as former player Luc Robitaille noted, after the NHL cancelled the 2004-2005 season because of a labor dispute.

That charge made Crosby stand out as a rookie, even on a team captained by Penguins legend Mario Lemieux.

"I guess the media always looked at him as different, sort of mature, and the rest of the world viewed him as a super child," Malone said. "The first day I met him, he just seemed like a normal human being."

Very little about Crosby seemed normal on the ice from his debut practice with the Penguins, who selected him first overall in 2005.

"He saw things other guys didn't and could do things other guys couldn't," former teammate and road roommate Ryan Whitney said. "It was sick. Five minutes in, you knew everything you heard about the guy was dead-on."

Away from the rink, Crosby impressed teammates with his ability to be "one of the guys," despite obvious differences such as a Canadian reporter chronicling his every move for a book about his rookie experience.

"He was a pretty normal kid — really humble," Penguins defenseman Brooks Orpik said. "I'm talking off the ice. On it, you could see right away that he was super competitive, driven and hated to lose. Those qualities are what I think made people think of him as a leader, even when he was a rookie."

"What's so special about him? I don't see anything special there. If you take any player, even if he is dead wood, and start promoting him, you'll get a star."
— Washington LW Alexander Semin, in an Oct. 31 interview with yahoosports.com

Hockey great Wayne Gretzky once predicted Crosby could break all 61 of his NHL records.

"He won't, and I know Wayne said it, but he won't," said Robitaille, the all-time leading scorer among NHL left wings. "But Sid got off to a pretty good start, didn't he?"

As a rookie at 18 Crosby was the youngest player to reach the 100-point plateau. As a sophomore at 19 he was voted the league's best player by his peers. Last season, he became the youngest captain in league history at 20, and he returned from a mid-season right ankle injury to finish tied for the playoff scoring lead as the Penguins advanced to the Stanley Cup final.

Crosby once described hockey as his great passion — his way of explaining the mere two weeks he takes off every summer.

Over the past few winters, though, a teammate and a nemesis have become breakout characters in a league once tabbed as "The Crosby Show."

"He hasn't taken a step back — Ovechkin and Malkin have picked it up," said Robitaille, now president of business operations with the Los Angeles Kings. "Sid's biggest sin is that there are three of these guys that are that amazing."

No lower than third in the scoring race since November, Crosby remains noticeably absent from MVP discussion that focuses on Malkin and Ovechkin.

"I was the second-leading scorer in the league when I got hurt," Crosby said of his recent four-game absence due to a groin injury.

"I would like to play a little bit better, but I don't think it was awful, either."

Through Wednesday, Crosby rated second in assists, even-strength points, road points and division points — despite missing five games because of injuries. He and Ovechkin were tied for second with a point-per-game average of 1.32, only slightly off Crosby's 1.37 career mark, which rates fifth-best in league history.

"He's earned the pressure — that's how I look at it with Sidney," Robitaille said. "I don't look at the pressure as being a bad thing because it means people expect great things from you."

"In the case of Sidney Crosby ... sometimes I wonder if he's having much fun."
— NBC analyst Mike Milbury, during a Feb. 22 national broadcast of a game between the Penguins and Capitals

Playing and leading is a lot more fun when the team is winning.

"I haven't changed what I've done from last year to this year," Crosby said. "With success, everything is a little bit easier, and sometimes people look for negative things as much as they look for positive things."

First-year Chicago Blackhawks captain Jonathan Toews, 20, agreed with Crosby.

"I'm one of those guys whose job is easier because we're winning," said Toews, whose team is ready to end a long playoff drought. "The success Sidney had as a young leader in Pittsburgh, even before he was captain, made it an easier decision to put young guys, myself included, into leadership roles."

The Penguins stopped winning regularly late in November.

Their struggles cost coach Michel Therrien his job Feb. 15.

Therrien said the very first decision he made upon replacing Eddie Olczyk as coach in December 2005 remains one of his proudest. He named Crosby, then a rookie, an alternate captain.

Therrien also recently dismissed speculation of a rift with Crosby.

"There were no problems between me and Sid or between Sid and his teammates," Therrien said. "He hates to lose. We were losing more than we expected, and he hated it — you could see it on his face."

Therrien said Crosby was and is "the perfect choice to be the captain of that young team."

"People forget how young some of those players are because they were so good so fast," Therrien said of the Penguins, whose top three forwards in terms of ice-time are Crosby, Malkin and center Jordan Staal, 20.

"Even Sid is still young. People get tired of hearing that, but it's the truth. He's probably the best player in the world most nights, but he's also only 21."

Crosby is younger than University of Pittsburgh basketball stars Sam Young, 23, and Levance Fields, 21 in June, and top Pirates prospects Pedro Alvarez and Andrew McCutchen, each 22.

"His situation is so different than anybody in any sport," Toews said of Crosby. "He's a young captain that also shoulders the responsibility of being the guy that is out there selling hockey around the world, not just in Pittsburgh.

"I don't think any young player has been asked to do as much as Sid. That probably makes his job more difficult. A lot of young guys get time to adjust and develop. Sid has had to be Sidney Crosby for a long time."

"I hate to say this, but maybe Sidney Crosby shouldn't be the captain of this team. Maybe he is too young and isn't the type to stand up and take charge."

— Penguins fan Beth Wellhausen of Bethel Park

Privately, Penguins teammates are worried about Crosby amid the criticism.

"I don't know what people — the media, some fans — are talking about," Penguins forward Max Talbot said last month. "He's our captain. He was our captain last season, and we almost won the Stanley Cup. Maybe so far this year we haven't lived up to our expectations, but you can't blame that on Sid."

Everything about Crosby — from his living arrangement with team co-owner Lemieux to on-ice wars of words with Ovechkin — has come under scrutiny.

"That's natural, that's what happens when you're a captain," Crosby said.

Goalie Marc-Andre Fleury said recently that people are "blaming Sid" for the Penguins' fall from grace this season.

"He wears the big target because of who he is," Fleury said. "He keeps us from taking a lot of the shots, but they all hit him."

Dallas' Modano knows that drill.

A Minnesota high-school star drafted at 18 in 1988 by his home-state North Stars, Modano acknowledged "a long period of feeling I was responsible for everything good and bad involving my team" that lasted through the franchise's relocation and ended only with its Cup win in 1999.

"I could tell him to miniaturize his goals and take everything on a day-by-day basis, but the big thing for him — because this was it for me — is to remember that this is a game, and it's supposed to be fun," Modano said. "At that age, though, it's hard to think like that.

"I'd tell Sid to be patient, because all this criticism will turn for him ... and it will be a lot more gratifying when it does because of all this he's going through now."

GREAT EXPECTATIONS

○ ○ ○ ○ ○

Penguins center Sidney Crosby, 21, may not be on pace to "break all of (Wayne Gretzky's) records," as Gretzky once predicted. However, through almost four full seasons, Crosby is trekking toward elite company. A look at where Crosby would rank all-time in points if he maintains his current per-game rate (1.37) for 1,000 more games:

Most NHL points

Player	Points	Games	PPG
Wayne Gretzky:	2,857	1,487	1.92
Mark Messier:	1,887	1,756	1.07
Gordie Howe:	1,850	1,767	1.05
Ron Francis:	1,798	1,731	1.04
Marcel Dionne:	1,771	1,348	1.31
*Sidney Crosby:	1,743	1,273	1.37

*—Projections based off statistics through Wednesday.
Source: NHL Guide and Record Book

Chaz Palla /Trib Total Media

Thrashers goaltender Johan Hedberg watches as Penguins forward **Evgeni Malkin** flips the puck to his backhand on a third-period penalty shot.

Chaz Palla photos/Trib Total Media

MALKIN COMES ALIVE IN PENGUINS' VICTORY

By Rob Rossi/TRIB TOTAL MEDIA

○ ○ ○ ○ ○

Wednesday, March 18, 2009

The shelf life of Penguins center Evgeni Malkin's nickname, "Geno," is short. In about three weeks, people can probably start calling him "Art."

"No, no, there are 10 games to go," Malkin said Tuesday after he tied a personal best with five points in the Penguins' 6-2 romp over the Atlanta Thrashers at Mellon Arena.

"(Call me) 'Geno' for a few more weeks. It's not done."

It is the NHL scoring race, and Malkin took five big strides toward the finish line last night. With two goals, his 31st and 32nd, and three assists, he pushed his league-best point total to 102.

Next closest among scorers is teammate and fellow star center Sidney Crosby, who recorded two assists last night. Crosby has scored 92 points — 13 in seven games since missing four straight with a groin injury.

One of the "Mega Powers" could deliver the Penguins their 13th scoring title in 21 seasons. If Malkin is that one, he will join Crosby, Jaromir Jagr (five) and Mario Lemieux (six) in Penguins lore.

Crosby and Jagr (once each) and Lemieux (three) also have won the Hart Trophy as league MVP.

With the resurgent Penguins (38-26-8, 84 points) on a

9-0-2 run that has made a once doubtful third consecutive Stanley Cup playoff berth seem likely, either Malkin or Crosby could claim the Hart.

Crosby, who won it and the scoring title in 2007, agreed last night that his and Malkin's chances are hurt by their standing as teammates.

"Yeah, that's probably true," Crosby said. "When you have guys 1-2 (in the scoring race), it's a bit of an argument there."

That argument is one that select members of the Professional Hockey Writers' Association might have if the Penguins hold their current fifth-place standing in the Eastern Conference.

Since interim coach Dan Bylsma replaced Michel Therrien on Feb. 15, the Penguins have gone from 10th-place and five points from a playoff spot to a six-point lead over ninth-place Florida.

Defenseman Sergei Gonchar scored his sixth goal and recorded three assists last night.

"I can't complain," said Gonchar, who has recorded 14 points in 15 games after missing the Penguins' first 56 contests because of a left-shoulder injury.

The Penguins, who went 3 for 6 on the power play, also received goals from left wing Chris Kunitz, his 22nd, center Jordan Staal, his 20th, and defenseman Mark Eaton, his third.

Gonchar refused to designate either Crosby or Malkin as more valuable.

"They're both outstanding players," Gonchar said. "I don't know how it will play out. I just know we are fortunate to have both playing for us."

The Hart Trophy is awarded to "the player adjudged to be most valuable to his team" as voted on by members of the PHWA.

Washington left wing Alex Ovechkin is considered a favorite to repeat as the winner. He bested Malkin for the scoring title and MVP last season after leading the Capitals to a Southeast Division title in the last week of the regular season.

Ovechkin is third in the NHL with 90 points and leads the league with 49 goals.

Several persons associated with the Penguins said last night they were not sure if the so-called teammate factor would hurt Malkin and/or Crosby in MVP voting.

"It's a good question ... I'm going to say, 'No,'" general manager Ray Shero said. "It shouldn't."

"It's hard to say," right wing Petr Sykora said. "People that vote understand hockey and they know how valuable those guys are for us. I don't think it should hurt them but ... you can't really say one of those guys is more valuable than the other.

"It's a hard decision to make."

Not for Crosby or Malkin.

"It's Sid," Malkin said. "He helps me. He makes good passes every game."

"When you look at that award, it's probably an award (for which) they look specifically at someone that really puts their team over and above," Crosby said. "He does that for us."

The Penguins' **Evgeni Malkin** scores the second of his two goals in the second period in front of the Thrashers' Boris Valabik (48) and Garnet Exelby.

PENGUINS COMPLETE PLAYOFFS COMEBACK

By Rob Rossi/TRIB TOTAL MEDIA

Wednesday, April 8, 2009

Penguins captain **Sidney Crosby** gets a shot past Tampa Bay Lightning goalie Karri Ramo for a power-play goal.

TAMPA — He is officially "The Dan that saved (their) season."

Goalie Marc-Andre Fleury coined that phrase Tuesday after the Penguins' 6-4 victory against the Tampa Bay Lightning at St. Pete Times Forum — a 16th win in 23 games under interim coach Dan Bylsma and the one that capped a stunning seven-week surge into the Stanley Cup playoffs.

Bylsma, who inherited a 10th-place club that was five points out of a playoff spot when he replaced former coach Michel Therrien on Feb. 15, passed "the majority of the credit to the guys in" a dressing room of relieved Penguins.

"We tried to play a certain way and we're still getting better at it," he said, referring to the Penguins' return to aggressive-styled hockey. "We're still not there yet, but we played the right way and it made for a remarkable turnaround."

The Penguins (43-28-9, 95 points) will be no worse than the No. 7 seed among an eight-team Eastern Conference playoff field. They are currently sixth, two points behind both Philadelphia and Carolina in a race for fourth-place and home-ice advantage in the first round.

After all they've overcome, right wing Petr Sykora said the Penguins are prepared to open defense of their conference crown wherever against whomever — and they'll like their chances to win a best-of-7 opening-round series.

"A lot of people were waiting for us to fail and not make the playoffs; to have two games left in the season and a playoff spot for this team — that's a huge achievement," Sykora said last night after his long-awaited 300th NHL goal (he had gone eight games without scoring) helped snuff out a spirited third-period rally by Tampa Bay.

"The second year after you have success, especially for a young team, is always hard. It's hard to come back, make the playoffs and make a run. Last year I felt very confident when we made the playoffs, and this year I feel confident we can do it again."

Aside from nearly blowing a four-goal lead last night, the Penguins have reason to be confident of a possible return to the Stanley Cup Final, where they lost in six games last season.

The biggest boost to their collective ego is the resurgence of captain Sidney Crosby as their best player.

Since missing four straight games with a groin injury, Crosby has tallied nine goals and recorded 22 points in 15 games.

His two goals last night pushed his point total to 101, third in the league. In his fourth season, Crosby owns three of the Penguins' league-record 100-point individual campaigns.

Oh, and Crosby's goals last night were power-play scores. He has three in four games after scoring only that many in 71 previous contests.

"I want to produce on the power play, I want to be a threat both passing and shooting, but sometimes you don't get the looks or put the puck in the net when you get chances," Crosby said. "It's the difference between three or four goals a year."

Crosby noted his high power-play goal production in junior hockey, where he "played a lot more on the goal line," as opposed to his customary spot on the half-wall, where he admits to "being more of a (passer) than a shooter."

"You want to be a threat both ways," Crosby said.

Crosby's 31st and 32nd goals keep Evgeni Malkin in the running to win his first Art Ross Trophy and deliver to the Penguins a 13th individual scoring title. Malkin assisted on each of Crosby's goals and leads Washington left wing Alexander Ovechkin, 110-108, in the point race.

Left wing Ruslan Fedotenko, whose 16th goal last night opened the scoring, said he and Sykora — Malkin's linemates for much of the past three months — are intent on helping him hold off Ovechkin.

"He's so good that he doesn't need a lot of help, but we need to do our part," Fedotenko said.

Center Jordan Staal has done his part since Bylsma arrived. His empty-net goal with 13 seconds remaining assured Tampa Bay could not win even with a fifth third-period goal.

With his 22nd goal and two assists, Staal has scored six goals and recorded 15 points since "The Dan" started the Penguins on this march.

"For a little bit we struggled and (the playoffs) were far away," Fleury said. "We had to stay confident and positive we could make it, and Dan made sure we did.

"Now we've made it, and we need to take a deep breath because we're going to have to play even better in the playoffs."

DAN BYLSMA

THE BOOK ON PENGUINS COACH BYLSMA

By Joe Starkey/TRIB TOTAL MEDIA

○ ○ ○ ○ ○

Sunday, April 12, 2009

Going back to his formative days in the Soviet Union, Penguins defenseman Sergei Gonchar has experienced coaches of every kind: the novice and the know-it-all; the curmudgeon and the coddler.

Surely, then, someone from Gonchar's past must remind him of his newest boss, Dan Bylsma.

Right?

Gonchar ponders the question, then seems to surprise himself with his answer.

"No," he says. "I don't think I had a guy like this before."

He wasn't the only one Bylsma surprised. The Penguins have posted an 18-3-4 record in Bylsma's first 25 games as "interim" coach, good for 40 points.

That represents one of the best coaching starts in NHL history.

Only three coaches, according to the Elias Sports Bureau, had posted as many as 40 points in their first 25 games: Todd McLellan had 43 with San Jose this season; Bep Guidolin had 40 with the 1972-73 Boston Bruins; and Pete Green had 40 with the original Ottawa Senators 90 years ago. Guidolin, like Bylsma, was hired during the season.

Bylsma, 38, owned a little less than four months professional head coaching experience when general manager Ray Shero summoned him Feb. 15 from the team's Wilkes-Barre farm club. Michel Therrien had been fired. The Penguins were five points out of a playoff position.

Bylsma is the youngest coach in the NHL, just a month-and-a-half older than Penguins right winger Bill Guerin. Yet, from his first moments on the job, he was a veritable Cool Dan Luke, behaving as if he was born for the role.

Those closest to him will tell you he was.

What follows is an attempt to answer perhaps the most popular question from the day the Penguins changed coaches: Who is Dan Bylsma?

DAN BYLSMA

HE IS THE FEISTY LITTLE BROTHER

By dad's orders, the Bylsma boys were forbidden to play tackle football at their home in Grand Haven, Mich.

Sure enough, when the boys violated orders one afternoon, something bad happened.

Seven-year-old Dan, youngest of the four, snapped his collarbone. But instead of yelling for help when his father came home from work, he tried to hide the injury.

"He wouldn't let on, because he didn't want anybody to get in trouble," recalled oldest brother Scott. "The bone was sticking out against the skin, and he didn't say anything."

Make no mistake: The fire that burns inside of Daniel Brian Bylsma was built and stoked by his position in a family that includes a younger sister, Laurie, and three successful older brothers — Scott, Greg and Jon.

Scott works at Merrill Lynch in Grand Rapids, near Grand Haven.

Jon is a corporate litigation attorney in Grand Rapids. Greg is the chief financial officer at Herman Miller, an office-furniture manufacturing company in Holland, Mich.

Dan was included in all their activities from the time he could walk.

OK, from the time he could crawl — and he never backed down from a challenge.

"If they wanted me to be all-time catcher, I was all-time catcher," Dan said. "They give the dirty work to the kid. That was me. I developed a work ethic and a tenacity because I was always trying to make up for a lack of size and skill. They were always better than me."

Not always. After each of the brothers either won a state golf championship or finished as runner-up at Western Michigan Christian High, Dan did them better: He won it as a freshman. He'll never forget jumping into Jon's arms after his winning putt.

That was part of a decorated, multi-sport athletic career that eventually would point Dan toward the NHL. Not that anything came easy.

He planned on becoming an accountant even into his senior year at Bowling Green State University.

The Winnipeg Jets had drafted Dan in the sixth round when he was a college freshman, prompting his dad to wonder, "What were they thinking?"

Dan interviewed with some top-six accounting firms his senior year, but the fire inside led him to try pro hockey. He began at the bottom — the East Coast League in 1992 — and clawed his way to the top, eventually becoming an alternate captain for the Western Conference champion Anaheim Ducks in 2003.

Here is a glimpse of Dan's singular focus, culled from a journal entry on Jan. 13, 1994, when he was playing for Moncton of the American Hockey League. He later published the entry in a book he co-wrote with father called, "So Your Son Wants to Play in the NHL."

"*Well, I finally signed the contract I've been waiting for: $35,000 Canadian. I'm waiting for next year's deal to come. ... Now my goals are reset for a new level, to the top, to the NHL. I know I can get there. It will happen. It is at the tip of my tongue, and it's so close I can almost taste it. And I will!*"

By the way, when a brotherly battle breaks out nowadays, it's little Dan who has the mental edge.

"He just has this confidence about him that he's going to win," Scott said. "He'll be losing, but he just knows. And you know, too. I've seen his body change when we're playing golf. One time I drubbed him on the front nine, and Dan just looked at me, and I knew I was going to lose.

"He won't tell you he's going to do it. But he's going to do it."

HE IS A HOCKEY LOVER

Baseball was Dan's best high-school sport — he played outfield on an all-state team that featured future Atlanta Braves pitcher Steve Avery — but hockey never strayed far from his heart.

He formed his gritty game on the backyard rink the Bylsma boys built every winter.

Jay, a certified public accountant who later managed companies and is a teacher at Grand Rapids Community College, grew up rooting for the Detroit Red Wings of Gordie Howe and Sid Abel.

He converted his basement into a "dressing room" for the boys, complete with locker stalls and an exterior wooden staircase that led to the ice surface. That way, his wife, Nancy, didn't have to deal with the daily mess.

The boys compared climbing those stairs to what players did at old Chicago Stadium. They'd yell, "Here come the Hawks!" as they emerged from the basement.

The pick-up games, of course, were ferocious. Often, it was just the four of them and their father battling under the floodlights until 11 p.m.

Jay was not an overbearing parent. Dan remembers coming home with a report card and his father simply asking, "Did you do your best?" When Dan said yes (good answer), his father congratulated him and left the manila envelope shut.

As detailed in, "So Your Son Wants to Play in the NHL," the first of four books Jay and Dan co-authored, Jay did not believe in focusing his children on a single sport, despite outside pressures.

Dan did not join a competitive travel team until he was 15. His father favored a varied experience, as does Dan with his son, 10-year-old Bryan.

Dan speaks to such issues — and many more involving youth sports — in various articles and question-and-answer sessions on his website, danbylsma.com.

The trick question for many parents, Dan believes, is when they hear a coach or other athletic authority figure ask, "Don't you want your child to have the best opportunity?"

"When I hear someone say that," Dan said, "my answer is, Absolutely. That's why he's going to play the guitar. That's why he's going to physics camp. That's why we're going to travel and see our family and do a lot of different things, because I know my priorities, and I know hockey's not the only damn thing in the world."

Jay did, however, encourage hard work and competition.

"We ate competitively," Jay said. "But after we'd play (on the outdoor rink), there was no talk of who'd won or who'd lost. We would just sit there in the basement, steam coming off our bodies, nobody saying a word. Just absorbing the moment."

HE IS THE VETERAN OF 429 NHL GAMES

Matt Cooke is one of several Penguins who played against Bylsma.

Ever run into him? "That's why I still wear this brace on my right knee," Cooke said, pulling up his pant leg after a recent practice. "He got me."

Apparently, as Cooke went to retrieve a puck, one of his defensemen failed to shield him from the raging bull that was the 6-foot-2, 215-pound Bylsma.

"I say it was a late hit," Cooke said, laughing. "(Bylsma) just says, 'It might have been a little late.'"

The book on Bylsma was that he wasn't ultra-talented (19 career goals) but would sacrifice a body part to win a game. He almost did on several occasions, too, including the time a shot crushed his orbital bone like an egg shell during a 1999 International League playoff game in Houston.

Playing for the Long Beach Ice Dogs, Bylsma went to one knee to block the shot. A decade later, he still has not regained his original smile. Nerve damage did that. His face was broken in 11 places and required 115 stitches and 13 pieces of metal to mend.

Bylsma still has two metal plates and six screws in his face.

"I wasn't there, but I saw the pictures," his father recalled. "You couldn't identify him. Several people called, including someone who was sitting by the glass. He told me, 'I thought he was going to die.'"

Early in Bylsma's Bowling Green career, he was demoted to the third line. That became his ticket to the NHL, as it forced him to learn the defensive side of the game. He became a master penalty killer. One of his future coaches, Larry Robinson, said Bylsma might have been the best penalty killing shot blocker in the league.

The proof is in the stitching. Ask Bylsma how many stitches and broken bones he sustained, and he will tell you he lost count at 550 and 26, respectively.

HE IS A DEVOTED FATHER

Bylsma is living out of a hotel while his wife, Mary Beth, and Bryan finish the school year in Wilkes-Barre. His office is decorated with Bryan's art work and notes of encouragement.

One crayon drawing simply says, "Olive Juice." Bylsma said if you look in the mirror and say, "Olive Juice," it looks like, "I love you." Being that it's not always cool for sons to use that expression with fathers, the two have their code phrase ready.

Bryan was a precious gift to Dan and Mary Beth, coming, as he did, shortly after the stillborn birth of their daughter. Bylsma was playing for the Los Angeles Kings at the time — Jan. 13, 1998. It had been a smooth pregnancy, so he was excited when he was summoned from the practice rink to take a call from his wife, who was 39 weeks pregnant.

Instead, it was the worst moment of his life. Their daughter had inexplicably passed away.

"I look back at that, and I don't know if I can say anything in words that will make sense to the average person," Bylsma said. "I just know my family and friends and upbringing were a huge part of getting through it."

Dan and his father were about to have their first book published. They decided to include the story of Dan's daughter as a way of demonstrating how one survives difficult times through perseverance, faith and a solid support system.

"Mary Beth and I and the nurse and doctor were the only four people who saw our child," Bylsma told the Citizen's Voice of Wilkes-Barre. "My dad didn't. My brothers didn't. My friends didn't. But to us, she's real.

"We wanted to share our experience."

HE IS DIFFERENT KIND OF COACH

Does Bylsma believe he was meant to be a coach, meant to be here? He isn't inclined to answer the question at the moment. But, he says, "If you ask me that when my coaching career is done, I'll definitely tell you yes."

Older brother Scott could see a budding coach decades ago. Penguins winger Petr Sykora saw it during his time as a teammate of Bylsma's in Anaheim. Sykora remembers a guy who wasn't afraid to stand up and address the team in an honest and direct fashion.

"Every coach is different," Sykora said. "I had a coach I didn't talk to for two years. Then you have others who are very open — Larry Robinson, Slava Fetisov, Danny. There's nothing really hidden there. I think that's the right way to do it."

Rarely does Bylsma feel compelled to raise his voice. He is more focused, he said, on teaching and creating an environment in which players are challenged daily.

Players seem to appreciate Bylsma's positive and creative approach. He dishes a healthy dose of sarcasm and is known to dedicate a practice to specific skills such as saucer passes and shot-blocking technique (rule No. 1: don't lead with your face).

"When you walk by his office, he'll say, 'Good morning,'" said defenseman Hal Gill. "He's a normal guy. There's no barrier at all."

A compulsive note taker in the mold of the late "Badger" Bob Johnson, Bylsma has books filled with his learnings. Jay Bylsma remembers his son returning home from Bowling Green after his freshman year hauling a stack of papers (papers he saved to this day).

"These are drills," Dan told him. "I'd like to be a coach someday."

Bylsma's major influences include Robinson, current St. Louis Blues coach Andy Murray, Blues assistant Brad Shaw, San Jose Sharks assistant coach Todd Richards and Detroit Red Wings coach Mike Babcock, who coached Bylsma in Anaheim and has exchanged a few texts with him since Bylsma got the Penguins job.

It was then-Wilkes-Barre coach Richards who brought Bylsma into the Penguins organization as an assistant three years ago.

Bylsma, who began his coaching career with the AHL's Cincinnati Ducks in 2004, had spent the previous season as an assistant with the New York Islanders. Richards chose him from among several candidates, based on a phone interview and a recommendation from Penguins assistant general manager Chuck Fletcher.

That is looking like a brilliant move at the moment, though Bylsma has not yet been tested in the crucible of playoff hockey. He hasn't been given the job yet, either, as the Penguins plan to wait until after the playoffs to evaluate the situation.

Might be the easiest decision they'll ever make.

DAN BYLSMA

TOPPING THE LIST

Dan Bylsma is off to the best start of any coach in Penguins history. Here are the best and worst 25-game starts in franchise history:

BEST
- Dan Bylsma: 2009 — 18-3-4 (40 pts)
- Gene Ubriaco: 1988 — 15-10-0 (30 pts)
- Scotty Bowman: 1991 — 13-8-4 (30 pts)

WORST
- Lou Angotti: 1983 — 4-16-5 (13 pts)
- Michel Therrien: 2005-06 — 4-15-6 (14 pts)
- Eddie Olczyk: 2003 — 6-15-4 (16 pts)

HISTORY MAKERS

Dan Bylsma tied the second-best 25-game start in NHL history.

Top Four

Todd McLellan:
San Jose Sharks, 2008-09, 21-3-1 (43 pts)

Bep Guidolin:
Boston Bruins, 1972-73, 20-5-0 (40 pts)

Pete Green:
Ottawa Senators, 1919-20-21, 20-5-0 (40 pts)

Dan Bylsma:
Penguins, 2008-09, 18-3-4 (40 pts)

Source: Elias Sports Bureau

FIVE QUICK QUESTIONS FOR BYLSMA

1. You get two tickets to a concert; any performer who ever lived. Who do you see?

"Ever lived? Wow. That's a tough question. I think the Beatles and their phenomenon and what they did to the music industry is something I would like to have seen. Elvis goes into that category, too, but I'll go with the Beatles."

2. You can have dinner with anyone on earth. Who?

"I think a day in the life of President Obama would be fascinating. I don't want to sit down and have dinner with him; I'd rather be on his shoulder and in his brain while he goes through his day, his week. If you're going to make me go to dinner, let's go play golf — a foursome with Tiger, Jack (Nicklaus) and Arnold Palmer. That would be a better thing: a round of golf and dinner."

3. What is your favorite movie?

"The 'Shawshank Redemption,' without question. I loved 'Braveheart' and 'Gladiator,' too. Those are my top three."

4. What is your favorite book?

"It changes pretty much every time I read one. I try to read a lot. I think I read 10 books in the past year. That's the one thing I do where I can continually educate my brain. (Bylsma goes to the bookshelf in his Mellon Arena office and pulls down Malcolm Gladwell's 'Outliers: The Story of Success.'). This is the same guy who wrote 'The Tipping Point' and 'Blink.' 'Blink' is about making split decisions and gut reactions and those types of things; what goes into that; why you do it. For a long time, my favorite book was 'The Bourne Identity,' along with 'The Bourne Supremacy' and 'The Bourne Ultimatum.'"

5. Growing up, who was your favorite athlete?

"My favorite hockey player was Wayne Gretzky, but my favorite athlete was (Detroit Tigers outfielder) Kirk Gibson. For a long time I kept a picture of him in my wallet. When I was playing high school baseball, I hung a poster of him in our dugout. It was him hitting a (World Series-clinching) home run in 1985, a laminated front page of the (Detroit) Free Press."

Penguins coach **Dan Bylsma's** calm demeanor is something that has rubbed off on his players.

Penguins coach **Dan Bylsma** and general manger **Ray Shero** share a lighter moment during a Stanley Cup Final press conference.

Christopher Horner photos/Trib Total Media

PENGUINS CONFIDENT HEADING INTO PLAYOFFS

By Rob Rossi/TRIB TOTAL MEDIA

○ ○ ○ ○ ○

Monday, April 13, 2009

Penguins defenseman Brooks Orpik "can't even remember back to a year ago."

A quick refresher: The Penguins, stoked by a second-half surge, entered the Stanley Cup playoffs as the Eastern Conference's No. 2 seed, believing they were built for a long postseason run.

Not everybody agreed with them.

"We thought we could win, but we really hadn't won anything in the playoffs to back that up; it was just a good feeling by guys in our room that we could win," Orpik said Saturday before the Penguins' 3-1 win at Montreal, which set up a first-round showdown with the Philadelphia Flyers — a rematch of the 2008 East Conference final.

Despite their seeding and a lineup that included star scoring centers Evgeni Malkin and Sidney Crosby and winger Marian Hossa, the Penguins were not forecasted to win the East, let alone go 12-2 en route to the Cup final.

In fact, some puck pundits wondered aloud and in print if the Penguins could slay their personal dragon, the Ottawa Senators, in the first round — even though the Senators entered the playoffs cooler than an Orange Julius.

"We had confidence," center Jordan Staal said, "but I'd say our confidence this year is different."

Facing the Flyers should only enhance the Penguins' good vibes.

They are 17-12-1 against Philadelphia during the Sidney Crosby Era, including 7-6-1 at Wachovia Center — no small accomplishment considering the Penguins have won only 28 of 132 games, including playoffs, played in a city that has mostly shown them no brotherly love.

Also, the Penguins are 3-0 over the past two playoff seasons in series that open at Mellon Arena, and they'll play Games 1 and 2 of this one — and most important, a deciding Game 7 — at the Igloo. They went 3-0 at home against the Flyers last season to win the East final in five games.

Still, neither that recent success nor familiarity with the Flyers is the reason the Penguins, as Orpik said, "have (their) own expectations" to make another long playoff run.

Nope, the truth is, as Staal noted, the Penguins would have liked their chances against any playoff foe.

"Why not?" Staal said. "It's pretty obvious to everybody on this team that we're playing our best hockey right now.

"That is why we are confident."

Several recent statistical trends suggest the Penguins should be confident:

• Role-playing wingers Tyler Kennedy, Max Talbot, Matt Cooke and Pascal Dupuis have scored 38 percent of their goals (20 of 52) in 25 games under interim coach Dan Bylsma.

• Staal's seven goals and 18 points since Bylsma replaced former coach Michel Therrien on Feb. 15 represent 32 and 37 percent of his output in those respective categories. Staal has registered three or more shots in nine games with Bylsma, compared to 18 in 57 games with Therrien.

• Left wing Ruslan Fedotenko, a noted clutch playoff performer, finished the regular season with three goals and 10 points and a plus-9 rating in his final seven games.

• The seven players that comprise the defensive corps have combined for only 34 minus games in 145 played with Bylsma, or 23 percent. Those players produced 77 minus games in 270 played under Therrien, or 29 percent.

• Crosby, entering the playoffs at near 100-percent health for the first time in his career, scored 10 goals and recorded 24 points in 16 games after missing four in a row because of a groin injury. His new wingers, trade acquisitions Bill Guerin and Chris Kunitz, have combined for nine goals and 25 points over that span.

• Under Bylsma, the penalty kill is at 87.6 percent (99 of 113) and power play at 19.6 percent (22 for 112). The Penguins previously were 80.3 percent (188 of 234) on the penalty kill and 16.1 percent (40 for 248) on the power play.

• Top defenseman and power-play quarterback Sergei Gonchar is rested, having played only 25 games — recording 19 points — after missing 56 to start the season because of a left-shoulder injury.

• NHL scoring champion Malkin scored 31 percent of his goals (11 of 35) with Bylsma.

• Finally, goalie Marc-Andre Fleury proved durable and devastating from Jan. 6. In 39 appearances, he went 24-9-5 with a 2.53 goals-against average and a .918 save percentage. Fleury allowed two or fewer goals in 19 of those games.

"Confidence, by my definition, is having belief in the outcome of a future event," Bylsma said Saturday. "You get that ... through work, past success, positive identity about yourself, and we have all three of those things right now. We've earned the right to be confident with our play.

"We have every right to be positive about how we play and how we're going to play."

DIGGIN' ON DAN

The Penguins went 18-3-4 to close the season under interim coach Dan Bylsma. A deeper dig into those 25 games:

· 10-2-2 against playoff teams

· 10-1-1 at Mellon Arena

· 12 games with four or more goals, compared to 19 in 57 previous games

· No power-play goals allowed in 15 games, compared to 24 in 57 previous games

· More shots than opponents in 16 games, compared to 17 in 57 previous games

Source: NHL statistics, Penguins media relations

PLAYOFF PAIRINGS

First round (Best-of-7)

EASTERN CONFERENCE

No. 1 Boston vs. No. 8 Montreal
No. 2 Washington vs. No. 7 N.Y. Rangers
No. 3 New Jersey vs. No. 6 Carolina
No. 4 Penguins vs. No. 5 Philadelphia

WESTERN CONFERENCE

No. 1 San Jose vs. No. 8 Anaheim
No. 2 Detroit vs. No. 7 Columbus
No. 3 Vancouver vs. No. 6 St. Louis
No. 4 Chicago vs. No. 5 Calgary

Penguins defenseman **Brooks Orpik** will lead a confident team into its first-round series against the Philadelphia Flyers.

FLEURY OUTSTANDING, AS PENGUINS STUN FLYERS IN OT

By Rob Rossi/TRIB TOTAL MEDIA

○ ○ ○ ○ ○

Sunday, April 18, 2009

This, folks, is the reason Penguins general manager Ray Shero opted last July to pay his goalie big bucks and decided in early-March that his team needed some veteran juice.

Behind a 38-save performance by goaltender Marc-Andre Fleury and trade deadline-day acquisition winger Bill Guerin's two goals, the Penguins swiped a 3-2 victory Friday from the Philadelphia Flyers at Mellon Arena.

Guerin's second goal with 1:31 remaining in the first overtime — a two-man advantage tally — pushed the Penguins to a 2-0 lead in their best-of-7 Eastern Conference quarterfinal playoff series against the Flyers.

The series shifts to Philadelphia on Sunday afternoon for Game 3, followed by Game 4 on Tuesday night the Flyers are in the same home-ice hole they were in last May, when they dropped a five-game Eastern Conference final to the Penguins.

"To go to Philly with a 2-0 advantage is pretty big," Fleury said after a showing that teammate and Penguins defenseman Brooks Orpik said ranks up there with any the so-called "Flower" has turned in since he was selected first overall at the 2003 entry draft.

"All you can say about 'Flower' is that he makes the saves when we need them," Orpik said. "He's been doing it for a while now, so you kind of get used to it.

"He's become that goalie."

He might be a bargain at $5 million, his annual salary on a seven-year deal singed last summer. Fleury is 16-6 over his last two playoff seasons, and he has allowed two or fewer goals in 14 of those contests, including two in this series.

Fleury stopped 64 of 67 shots in Games 1 and 2.

At least a half-dozen of his saves last night prevented the Flyers from extending their lead to two goals — after they went ahead 1-0 on left wing Scott Hartnell's power-play tally in the first period and following center Darroll Powe's early third-period goal to give Philadelphia a 2-1 lead.

Guerin, acquired from the New York Islanders on March 4 for a conditional 2009 draft pick, scored his first playoff goal since 2006 — when he played for the Dallas Stars — with 3:22 remaining in the second period to pull the Penguins even, 1-1.

"It had been a while," Guerin said, before noting his new club's "incredible chemistry."

That stick-togetherness, which Orpik said fueled an 18-3-4 finish to the regular season under interim coach Dan Bylsma, was on full display during a late third-period power play that followed Flyers center Jeff Carter's hooking penalty.

NHL regular-season scoring leader Evgeni Malkin, working for positioning in front of the creased guarded by Flyers goalie Martin Biron, was credited with his second playoff goal after defenseman Kris Letang's point-shot caromed off his skate and across the goal line.

Malkin's goal with 3:37 remaining in regulation tied the score, 2-2, and was one of his three points. He has recorded five points in the series.

"The ice was not great and (the Flyers' penalty-kill units) apply a lot of pressure, so I just tried to get it to the net — especially after that great, between-the-legs pass by (Penguins defenseman Sergei Gonchar)," Letang said.

"It went off 'Geno,' but at that point, who cares, as long as it goes in."

About five minutes before Malkin scored, Carter was robbed by Fleury, whose sparkling skate-save resembled one he made last year during a 55-save effort in the Penguins' triple-overtime victory at Detroit in Game 5 of the Stanley Cup Final.

"That one was bigger because it was the Final," Orpik said, "but this one belongs with any he's ever made after that."

Philadelphia's Scott Hartnell works the puck past Penguins goaltender **Marc-Andre Fleury** for a power-play goal during the first period Friday at Mellon Arena.

BILL GUERIN

PENGUINS' GUERIN REFUSES TO ACT HIS AGE

By Rob Rossi/TRIB TOTAL MEDIA

○ ○ ○ ○ ○

Sunday, April 19, 2009

*I stood stonelike at midnight,
Suspended in my masquerade/
I combed my hair 'till it was just right,
And commanded the night brigade*

— Opening lyrics to Bruce Springsteen's "Growin' Up"

Luck had nothing to do with the two goals Penguins right wing Bill Guerin scored Friday, including an overtime winner, to lift his doesn't-feel-like-NEW-anymore club to a 2-0 lead in its best-of-7 Eastern Conference quarterfinal playoff series against Philadelphia.

As Guerin's center, Sidney Crosby, said hours after that Penguins' victory over the Flyers, those markers "were goal-scorer's goals" — shots equally precise and powerful.

Simply being around to take those shots, though, has Guerin feeling as though he is living the script for a character created by his favorite rocker, Bruce Springsteen.

"Yeah, that fits," Guerin said of a comparison to his time with the Penguins and Springsteen's latest single, "My Lucky Day."

"I just feel real good about being here."

The Penguins feel really good about their Stanley Cup chances, and they have since Wild Billy's Circus Story came to town.

HUNGRY HEART
○ ○ ○ ○ ○

Guerin joined the Penguins on March 5. He was acquired the previous afternoon from the New York Islanders, a rebuilding club whose captain hungered for the playoff excitement that comes from stepping onto the ice in front of a hostile crowd — as the Penguins will do this afternoon for Game 3 at Wachovia Center — and "getting booed so loud it feels good."

A Stanley Cup-winner with New Jersey in 1995, Guerin, not unlike any 38-year-old player, realized during his final season with the Islanders that: A) he wasn't getting any younger; B) they weren't getting any closer to competing for a championship; and, C) with his impending unrestricted free agency this summer, that relationship was on life-support.

BILL GUERIN

So, he agreed to pull the plug, waiving a no-trade clause to join the Penguins, whose general manager Ray Shero gleefully paid a conditional 2009 draft pick for a right-handed shooting winger with skill, grit and a reputably charming personality.

Well, maybe not by the traditional definition of charming ...

"The best stories I can tell about Billy, I can't tell," said Penguins defenseman Hal Gill, who played with Guerin as members of the Boston Bruins.

"He's not a guy that is uncomfortable in many situations, which is good — probably it's what we needed when he arrived, because there was a lot going on.

"He was, like, a perfect fit."

PROVE IT ALL NIGHT

Guerin joined the Penguins less than three weeks after interim coach Dan Bylsma replaced Michel Therrien and a week following the acquisition of left wing Chris Kunitz from Anaheim for popular defenseman Ryan Whitney.

The morning he met his new teammates, Guerin faced prepping for the Penguins' biggest game of the season — at Florida against the Panthers, whom they were chasing for a playoff spot.

"I met Billy at the (2007) All-Star Game in Dallas, so we knew each other a little bit," Crosby said. "His first day here, we were playing in Florida that night, and I remember shaking his hand, saying hello.

"A minute later, he ripped me about something. I don't remember what it was, but it took him all of a minute to (bust my chops)."

That was the Guerin his fellow Massachusettsian Gill assured Shero would "keep everybody loose" during a pressure-packed final five regular-season weeks.

"He has this presence," Shero said. "As soon as you meet him, you can feel it and see it.

"He's a great teammate, because Billy's just a great guy."

It took Guerin less than 24 hours to take the Penguins in a new direction. His one-touch pass through the neutral zone connected on the stick blade of a hard-charging Crosby, who split two Florida defenders and scored a breakaway goal in the Penguins' 4-1 victory.

The Penguins went 11-2-3 after that victory to earn the East's No. 4 seed and home-ice advantage in the first playoff round.

Guerin scored five goals and recorded 12 points in 17 regular-season games with the Penguins.

Perhaps more importantly, he and Kunitz sparked Crosby, who scored 10 goals and amassed 24 points over that span.

THE TIES THAT BIND

Those Penguins who knew Guerin only for his success with seven other clubs soon learned first-hand that his former Devils teammate, goalie Martin Brodeur, was hardly kidding upon insisting last month, "Billy will skate through a dozen walls for you."

Or, as Penguins center Max Talbot said earlier this week after Guerin's Game 1-ending fight with Flyers defenseman Braydon Coburn — a player 14 years Guerin's junior: "Billy's got a lot of (guts), and guys respect that."

"Oh, he's a very tough guy," hard-hitting Penguins defenseman Brooks Orpik said of Guerin. "I think with Billy, though, he's so smart at finding open space that he doesn't have to get himself beat up in front of the net to score goals.

"For a big and strong guy, he's really good at finding those small pockets in the offensive zone — and he's got that good shot, and he gets it off so quick, so as soon as there's a turnover, as a defenseman, you have to worry about Billy getting a one-timer, because he's always in position to shoot.

"And he can shoot."

POINT BLANK

Flyers goalie Martin Biron knows Guerin's shot all too well. The one that bested him Friday in the second period wowed Penguins goalie Marc-Andre Fleury — generally regarded as possessing the quickest reaction time among his peers.

"It looked pretty heavy, and I was at the other end," Fleury said of the shot that produced Guerin's first playoff goal since 2006. "I've seen him when he was on the other teams and now a lot in practice, and when he gets his shot, the goalie needs to make a great save to stop it from going in."

The way Guerin shoots — right-handed — has opened a world of possibilities for Crosby, arguably the sport's finest playmaker. Aside from former Penguins winger Colby Armstrong, who skated on Crosby's line for the final months of the 2005-06 campaign, Crosby has worked regular shifts with players that, like him, shoot lefty.

"It's great for breakouts and making plays around the blueline — things that wouldn't seem like much, but since it's so natural for him being on his strong side, it makes little plays that much easier," Crosby said of Guerin, who has scored 408 goals.

"He's made a living for a number of years being a sniper. He's got a great shot, and year after year, he's proven he can score goals. Since he's come to us, it's been the same thing.

"Billy is a dangerous guy out there, and we've been a dangerous team with him."

LUCKY MAN

Guerin's favorite Springsteen lyric is from one of The Boss' earliest songs, "Growin' Up."

That title, Guerin admits, speaks to his child-like enthusiasm for life and its pleasures, which for him include a big family and, ideally, a few more seasons in the league.

He'll be free to leave the Penguins on July 1, and 39 on Nov. 9 — the latter an unavoidable fact that likely will keep Shero from offering him a long-term contract.

Shero's policy is not to discuss contract matters concerning any player during the playoffs.

"And I don't want to talk about it right now," Guerin said. "There are bigger things going on, and I want to stay focused on that.

"Everybody wants to know about next year, but I'm just trying to enjoy the present. I'm so glad that it worked out, and I'm here in Pittsburgh right now.

"I'm fortunate. I'm lucky."

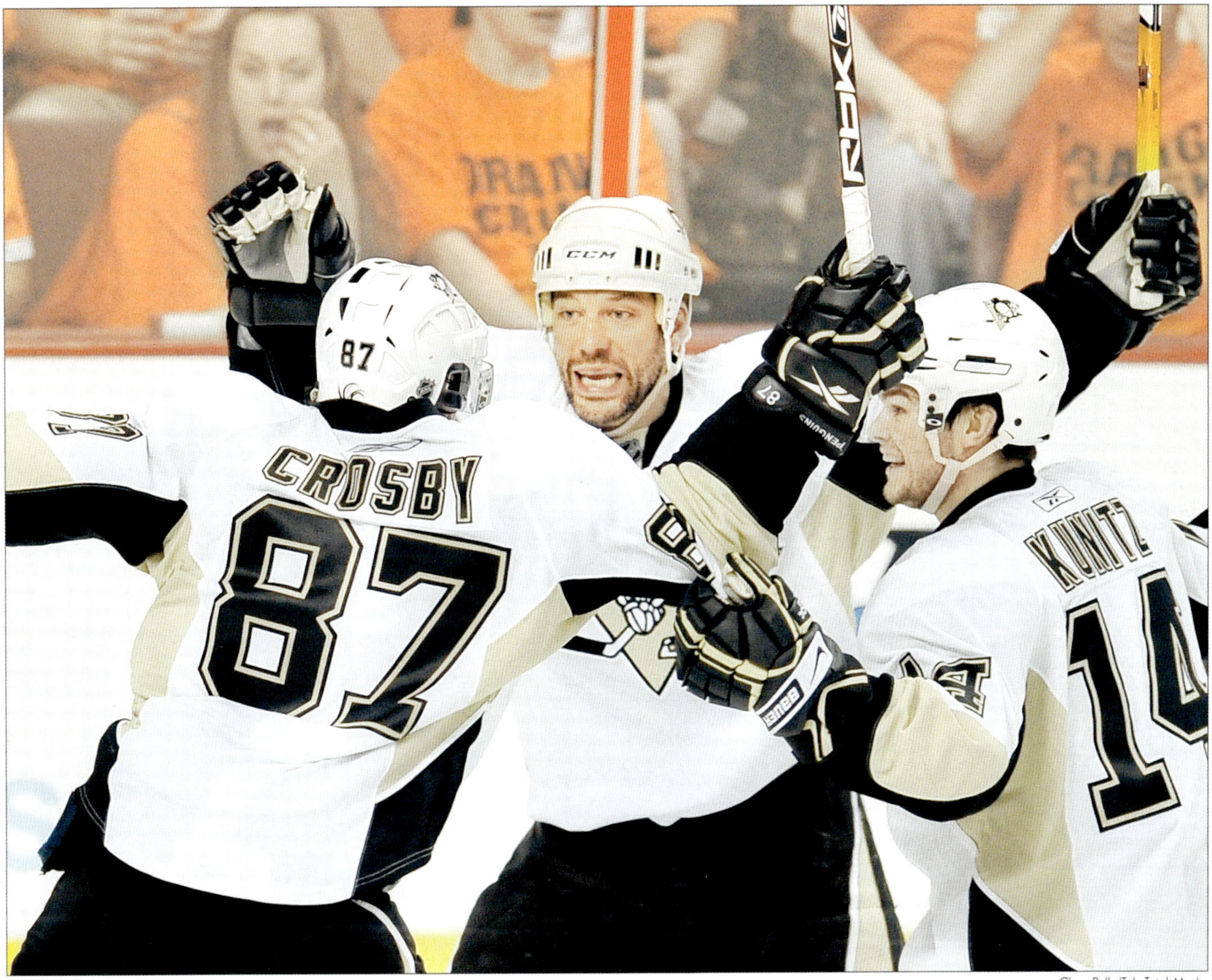

Chaz Palla/Trib Total Media

Penguins **Bill Guerin** and **Chris Kunitz** celebrate **Sidney Crosby's** second-period goal to tie the Flyers.

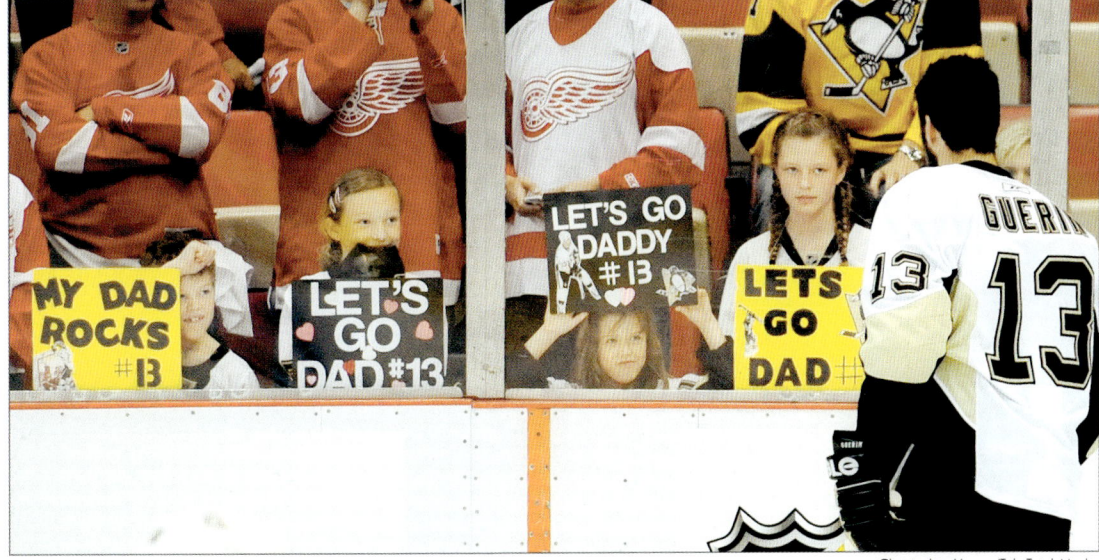

Penguins winger **Bill Guerin** skates past his kids during warm-ups before Game 5 of the Stanley Cup Final.

Christopher Horner/Trib Total Media

Penguins goaltender **Marc-Andre Fleury** makes a second-period glove save against the Flyers in Game 4 at the Wachovia Center.

FLEURY SENSATIONAL AS PENS HOLD OFF FLYERS

By Rob Rossi/TRIB TOTAL MEDIA

○ ○ ○ ○ ○

Wednesday, April 22, 2009

PHILADELPHIA — From Marc-Andre Fleury to the Philadelphia Flyers: "Thanks."

Hours after learning the Flyers claimed to have figured him out, Fleury — "our go-to guy ... the first star of the game, and maybe (all three)," as center Max Talbot said — stopped 45 shots Tuesday night in his club's 3-1 victory at Wachovia Center, giving the Penguins a commanding 3-1 lead in this best-of-7 first-round playoff series.

"It worked out pretty well," Fleury said, responding to early-morning comments from Flyers right wing Joffrey Lupul that the Penguins' goaltender was beatable with "an extra pass, an extra move" because he was playing "a long way out of the net."

Fleury listened to those words and spent yesterday afternoon watching video from the Penguins' Game 3 loss in which he allowed five goals on 29 shots — a stunning turnaround from his 64 saves on 67 shots in Games 1 and 2 at Mellon Arena.

"I thought about those guys holding onto the pucks," Fleury said, later, adding that maybe the Flyers' critique was correct.

"They were right a little bit. Maybe they shouldn't have said anything."

Had they not, perhaps the Flyers would have swept two games at home and returned to Mellon Arena on Thursday for Game 5 with the series tied.

Instead, the Penguins can advance to the second round for a second consecutive season with a victory at home, where they are 5-0 against the Flyers in the playoffs over the past two seasons.

Fleury's teammates credit him after a showing that captain Sidney Crosby called "pretty similar" to his 55-save showstopper in a triple-overtime Game 5 victory at Detroit in the 2008 Stanley Cup Final.

Flyers coach John Stevens and his players realized after the pivotal game last night which player was responsible for them facing playoff elimination.

"He was unbelievable," defenseman Kimmo Timonen said. "We pretty much threw everything at him."

"I told them, 'You can't let him continue to outwork us,'" Stevens said. "I don't want to say he outworked us, but he beat us because we only got one puck in the net."

That puck was shot by former Penguins' prospect and left wing Daniel Carcillo, whose first goal with the Flyers at 11:44 of the third period came on his club's 39th shot.

That was a stark contrast to Game 3, when the Flyers scored on their initial two shots.

The Penguins managed only 26 shots, but two of them bested Flyers goalie Martin Biron. Crosby and right wing Tyler Kennedy each scored their second goals of the playoffs in the second period, and Talbot's first into an empty net with 52 seconds remaining in regulation sealed the victory.

Crosby's goal was disputed by the Flyers' Stevens, but it was a "typical (Crosby) goal," according to Penguins interim coach Dan Bylsma.

After the Penguins killed an early second-period Flyers power play — one of a perfect 8-for-8 effort — Crosby drove hard toward Philadelphia's cage and was credited with a goal after a crossing pass from left wing Chris Kunitz deflected off his stick and body and past the Flyers' Biron.

The Penguins led, 1-0, at 3:19.

"'Kuni' just put it over the defenseman, sliding it," Crosby said. "I think I got my backhand on it. I'm not sure if it went off me after that or what, but I know I got my stick on it."

"That's how he scores most of his goals," Bylsma said. "When he's effective, he's forcing teams to deal with his speed going to the blue paint."

Fleury, Talbot said, is most effective when his competitive blood, often overshadowed by his easy-going demeanor, starts to boil.

"When you challenge him, know what to expect," Talbot said. "He's been a force for us. He's been that for us the last couple of years."

He was that last night, and then some.

FIVE-GOAL BARRAGE LIFTS PENS TO NEXT ROUND

By Rob Rossi/TRIB TOTAL MEDIA

Sunday, April 26, 2009

Linesman Jay Sharrers escorts Penguins center **Max Talbot** off the ice as Talbot gestures to the crowd during Game 6 action at the Wachovia Center.

PHILADELPHIA — Once again the Penguins have ended their archrival's hockey season, and center Max Talbot was quite willing late Saturday afternoon to tell the tale of this triumph.

"It was my fault the Flyers scored that goal late in the first period ... and they turned that into a 2-0 lead after we dominated the period," Talbot said after the Penguins' series-clinching 5-3 victory over Philadelphia at Wachovia Center. "I was pretty discouraged. You could see it on my face. I'm sitting on the bench before the second period is about to start, my head down, and (Sidney Crosby) comes up to me and says, 'Don't worry, Max; I'm going to get that one back for you.'

"That look in his eyes, that seriousness in his voice — I knew he would do what he said, and I knew we'd end up winning the game."

Flyers fans are wrong. Penguins captain Sidney Crosby doesn't "(stink)."

He scored twice yesterday — a tying goal late in the second period to erase the Flyers' three-goal lead, and an empty-net score to drive the final nail into their coffin — and the Penguins won this best-of-7 Eastern Conference quarterfinal playoff series, 4-2.

Defenseman Sergei Gonchar's slap-shot blast at 2:19 of the third period sent the Penguins into Round 2 for a second consecutive season. It also capped a comeback from a 3-0 deficit — a sweet celebration of a one-year anniversary from a previous franchise-best postseason rally.

The Penguins trailed the New York Rangers, 3-0, in Game 1 of an East semifinal series on April 25, 2008. They won that game, 5-4, on their way to the Stanley Cup Final — and maybe they are on their way back this season.

Crosby, whose four goals in the series matched fellow star center Evgeni Malkin's total, knows now is not the time to think about playing for the Cup again. Heck, the Penguins don't know the identity of their next-round opponent yet.

However, their rally yesterday to win a second road playoff game convinced Crosby that anything is possible for his resilient club.

"We just believe in each other," he said. "All those experiences you go through build trust, and we have that."

They also had a distinct territorial advantage in the first period yesterday, though they trailed after it, 2-0, on late goals by Flyers wingers Mike Knuble and Joffrey Lupul.

Talbot took blame for Knuble's second goal of the playoffs, scored at 17:48 of the first period after Flyers center Mike Richards stripped Talbot of the puck inside the Penguins' defensive zone. Only 51 seconds later, Lupul ripped a shot past Penguins goalie Marc-Andre Fleury to give the Flyers a two-goal cushion.

"We felt we played a good first period, and it kind of got away from us," Penguins interim coach Dan Bylsma said.

Bylsma's club had failed to score on no fewer than eight quality scoring chances by the time Flyers center Daniel Briere's power-play goal at 4:06 of the second period staked Philadelphia to a 3-0 lead.

Flyers general manager Paul Holmgren was restless from his suite.

"It's not like they're the Little Sisters of the Poor," he said of the Penguins. "I wasn't comfortable when it was 3-0 because they're a dangerous team."

Yep, the Penguins literally had some fight left — especially facing a possible deciding Game 7 at Mellon Arena on Monday.

Talbot challenged noted Flyers enforcer Daniel Carcillo to a fight 15 seconds after Briere's goal. He lost that battle, but fighting it helped win the Penguins this Commonwealth Cold War.

"He really changed momentum," Bylsma said. "That started us, and we kept on going."

The Penguins pulled to within 3-1 at 4:35 on left wing Ruslan Fedotenko's crease-crashing goal, his first of the playoffs. Defenseman Mark Eaton swatted past Flyers goalie Martin Biron a rebound off Penguins right wing Tyler Kennedy's shot at 6:32 — and Philadelphia's lead was cut to 3-2.

Crosby buried his third goal of the series behind Biron at 16:59, and a once-frenzied orange-clad mass at Wachovia Center turned furious fairly fast.

"They hate him here," Penguins winger Pascal Dupuis said. "I mean, they really hate him — chanting that he (stinks) every time he's on the ice, and even when he's not.

"They started it during ('God Bless America') today, and I kept thinking, 'Keep going, keep it up and make him want this even more.'

"I hope they ride him every time he comes here, because he takes inspiration from it."

Crosby's 20 goals in 26 regular-season games against the Flyers are his best against any club. He has scored six in 11 playoff games against the Flyers, who the Penguins ousted from the 2008 Eastern Conference final in five games.

Crosby admitted his two-goal performance yesterday was satisfying, though he hardly seemed overjoyed.

"He'll never show it too much," said Fleury, who stopped 22 shots. "Especially here, where they are really rough on him, it's a lot for him to score those two goals and end the series. I liked watching it. We all did.

"He's the man."

Dan Bylsma speaks to the media after being announced as the head coach of the Pittsburgh Penguins.

PENGUINS REMOVE BYLSMA'S INTERIM TAG

By Tricia Lafferty/TRIB TOTAL MEDIA

○ ○ ○ ○ ○

Wednesday, April 29, 2009

Thirty-one games into Dan Bylsma's NHL coaching career, the Penguins removed the interim tag and signed him to a three-year contract.

"It's weird because it looks like he's been coaching for 25 years," forward Pascal Dupuis said of Bylsma. "As soon as he walked in (on the first day), we felt he was confident and he knew what he was talking about. It was easy for everybody to see that."

Bylsma, 38, replaced former coach Michel Therrien on Feb. 15 and has turned a struggling Penguins squad into a club that Philadelphia Flyers chairman Ed Snider recently identified as a favorite to play in the Stanley Cup final.

Snider should know: Bylsma's Penguins eliminated the Flyers from the first-round of the 2009 Stanley Cup playoffs.

That accomplishment and the presence of the Penguins in the postseason — they were five points from the East's final playoff spot and 10th in the conference standings when Bylsma was promoted from AHL Wilkes-Barre — convinced Penguins general manager Ray Shero that Bylsma was his guy.

The Penguins finished the regular season on an 18-3-4 tear under Bylsma.

"It just became more and more evident to me and became clearer and clearer that Dan was the guy I really wanted to move forward with," Shero said. "I asked myself the question, 'Why wait?'"

Shero made his move three days after the Penguins eliminated the Flyers and hours before they learned of their second-round opponent. Beating a tough and talented Flyers team in six games — including a rally in Game 6 in which the Penguins came back from a 3-0 deficit — perhaps sealed the deal for Shero.

It capped Bylsma's already impressive tryout with a Penguins team that seemed reinvigorated under his watch.

"What I really like about Dan and we talked about this ... in a nutshell, Dan's approach is, when you're down, 3-0, our style of play to the players was just keep playing the right way," Shero said.

The detail-oriented, energy-filled Bylsma didn't think he'd be an NHL head coach at this point in his career. A little more than two months ago, he was 55 games into his first head coaching job with the Penguins AHL affiliate in Wilkes-Barre.

Then, he got the call to replace Therrien. The same night Bylsma accepted the promotion, Shero deemed him "one of the up-and-coming young coaches in this game."

Bylsma is the youngest coach in the NHL, which might explain why this ride has been surreal to him.

"When you hope and you have hopes and dreams about how you think it's going to go for you ..." Bylsma said. "It certainly happened quicker than I expected or could have expected or anyone expected."

His players didn't seem surprised after being told at a meeting Tuesday morning that Bylsma would be the coach to, as Shero put it, "grow with this team."

The players gushed over Bylsma's passion, work ethic and communication prowess.

"I think he's definitely proven that he knows how to coach a team," defenseman Hal Gill said. "He knows the psyche of a hockey player and he knows how to motivate. He's a young guy. I think he's got a great future."

Having played nine seasons in the NHL from 1995-2004, Bylsma isn't too far removed from the situation his players are in. Maybe that's why, as forward Bill Guerin said, being a great communicator is "probably Dan's biggest asset" and why his calmness during the playoffs "is something that's contagious."

It wasn't long ago that Bylsma was on the other side of the bench when he played in a Stanley Cup Final — in 2004 with Anaheim.

He had the same goals his players have and still does as a coach. They respect what he's done and where he's trying to lead them.

"That the guys respect him as a human being is the biggest thing," defenseman Brooks Orpik said. "I think the biggest thing is guys believe he's doing it for our benefit and not his."

Penguins coach **Dan Bylsma** never wavered from his message of playing the game the right way.

Christopher Horner/Trib Total Media

Penguins center **Sidney Crosby** scores a second-period goal past the Capitals' Simeon Varlamov during Game 2 of the Eastern Conference semifinal at the Verizon Center.

CROSBY, OVECHKIN TAKE CENTER STAGE IN EPIC BATTLE

By Tricia Lafferty/TRIB TOTAL MEDIA

○ ○ ○ ○ ○

Tuesday, May 5, 2009

WASHINGTON — Game 2 between the Penguins and the Washington Capitals was like watching a heavyweight fight.

Center Sidney Crosby and left wing Alex Ovechkin went punch for punch — or rather puck for puck.

Viewers weren't the only ones impressed by the double hat trick. The players skating alongside the superstars during the Capitals' 4-3 victory in the Eastern Conference semifinal Monday night at the Verizon Center seemed to be just as in awe of the show that rivals Crosby and Ovechkin produced.

They weren't surprised, though, with what two of the best players in the world had just accomplished.

"It's everything the media made it out to be," Capitals defenseman Mike Green said. "It's a battle of the two best players in hockey and (Monday night) they both carried their teams."

No players were campaigning for whose guy was better. They were just admiring how Crosby and Ovechkin went round for round, goal for goal. So far, the duo has combined for eight of the series' 12 goals.

"How they compete against each other, how they take it personal ... I'm just glad our man came out on top," Capitals center Brooks Laich said. "(Ovechkin is) a fun guy to play with. It just seems like pucks fly off his stick."

Ovechkin shined brighter last night only because his three goals lifted his team to victory. He scored two third-period goals to give the Capitals a two-goal advantage.

"Sick game," Ovechkin said. "Sick three goals by me and (Crosby). If I was a Capitals fan, I'd be very happy right now."

Crosby, understandably, was not thinking about his hat trick. He was instead focusing on how his team needs to rebound from an 0-2 start to the series.

"It's nice to score, but it's better to win," Crosby said.

In a matchup that was one of the most hyped second-round playoff series in recent history, Crosby and Ovechkin delivered.

"This time of year, you find out who the real players are," Laich said. "You find out who wants it. You find out who's having more fun. When the cameras are on is the moment the stars usually shine."

Crosby and Ovechkin combined for six goals last night. There were only seven through 60 minutes.

"They apparently heard the hype and are living up to it," Penguins coach Dan Bylsma said. "They're rising to the occasion."

Though Ovechkin and Evgeni Malkin are finalists for the Hart Trophy — awarded to the NHL's most valuable player — Crosby is proving he's still right up there with the league's best.

"Their guy played awesome, too," Laich said. "He's the reason they were in the game. It's awesome to see two guys battle back and forth in the same game."

The Penguins' **Evgeni Malkin** celebrates in front of fans after scoring against Washington during the third period of Game 3 of the Eastern Conference semifinals at Mellon Arena.

PENGUINS SOLVE CAPITALS IN OVERTIME

By Rob Rossi/TRIB TOTAL MEDIA

○ ○ ○ ○ ○

Thursday, May 7, 2009

Don't blink, or you might miss an adversity-tested team trying to do past Penguins clubs proud.

Second-year defenseman Kris Letang's first career playoff goal midway through an overtime period lifted the Penguins to a 3-2 victory Wednesday in Game 3 of a tight Eastern Conference semifinal playoff series against the Washington Capitals.

Each game has been decided by a goal, and the Penguins can pull even in the best-of-7 affair with another win Friday at Mellon Arena.

"It was desperation for us, obviously," Penguins center and captain Sidney Crosby said. "We're still in a similar position now, but we knew this was a big game."

It was a contest in which maligned center Evgeni Malkin performed as though he was driven to dominate after hearing and reading for days about his failure to score a goal in five consecutive games.

Regular-season scoring champions are expected to do better, especially when they will receive $8.7 million annually over five years starting next season.

Malkin's first goal of this series with 5:01 remaining in the third period — a whip-shot on a power-play chance that he drew — beat rookie Capitals goalie Simeon Varlamov (39 saves) and provided the Penguins with a 2-1 lead.

"He's a great player," Capitals defenseman Shaone Morrisonn said of Malkin, who was credited with nine shots (on 11 attempts) and two hits.

"He's going to get some chances. He capitalized."

The Capitals capitalized on an interference penalty committed by Penguins winger Pascal Dupuis at 17:32. Center Nicklas Backstrom's first playoff goal on a power play with 1:50 remaining tied the score, 2-2.

Down two games, that tally might have devastated any other team.

These Penguins aren't any other team. They're 12 months removed from playing in the Stanley Cup Final and about three from a coaching change that brought Dan Bylsma to Pittsburgh from AHL affiliate Wilkes-Barre.

The Penguins, 10th in the East and five points from a playoff spot upon Bylsma's hiring, finished the regular season on a 18-3-4 tear to earn a No. 4 playoff seed.

They were not about to blink at a two-game series deficit.

"Being down, 2-0, there could have been room to hang our heads," defenseman and respected dressing-room leader Brooks Orpik said. "More than anything, I think we were just disappointed that we kind of let a couple games slip away (at Washington). We scored first in both games, and not taking anything away from (the Capitals), but we kind of felt that we beat ourselves."

That was the case last night on Washington's first goal.

Capitals left wing Alex Ovechkin's eighth of the playoffs — and fifth of the series — staked his club to a 1-0 lead. Unlike his previous series scores, this one had little to do with Ovechkin's scary-sharp shot, which he used to record a hat trick in Game 2.

Capitals defenseman Mike Green fired the puck into the Penguins' zone from the neutral zone — essentially a hard dump-in, though one that left Penguins goalie Marc-Andre Fleury in the dumps.

Fleury left his goal crease to retrieve the puck. He lost his stick, and the puck ricocheted off the backboards and into the slot area in front of the cage. Ovechkin, unguarded, shot into an open net before Fleury, still sans paddle, could dive and attempt to grab it with his glove.

The Penguins pulled even, 1-1, at 9:29 of the second period. Left wing Ruslan Fedotenko's second playoff goal came after a 2-on-1 rush with Max Talbot, who worked the right wing on the Penguins' second line.

Fedotenko said he tried to lift a pass over backward-sliding Capitals defenseman Milan Jurcina. Instead, the puck bounced back to Fedotenko, who whipped it past Varlamov.

"I feel like we've put a lot of pucks on the net," Fedotenko said of the Penguins, who have averaged 35 regulation shots per game in the series. "We've created a lot of chances. One will go in eventually. We've just got to keep trying to throw the puck on the net and get some ugly ones."

Though none of these Capitals was part of seven previous playoff series between the teams, this loss reminded many of past post-season matchups.

The Penguins have won six of seven overtime playoff contests against Washington. They've also overcome two-game deficits on three occasions.

Perhaps that knowledge sparked the gleam in Penguins' majority co-owner Mario Lemieux's eyes as he stood in the dressing room and congratulated players.

After all, as Talbot said, "The series is on."

The Penguins celebrate **Kris Letang's** game-winning goal in overtime to beat the Capitals in Game 3 of the Eastern Conference Semifinal.

The Penguins' **Sidney Crosby** watches the puck elude Capitals rookie goaltender Simeon Varlamov for the game-winner in overtime.

PENS PUSH CAPITALS TO BRINK WITH OT VICTORY

By Rob Rossi/TRIB TOTAL MEDIA

○ ○ ○ ○ ○

Sunday, May 10, 2009

WASHINGTON — It's who they are.

There is no other way Penguins captain Sidney Crosby can explain his club, which over a span of about 15 third-period minutes Saturday pulled even, ahead and fell into a tie with the Washington Capitals — all without the services of steady-handed defenseman Sergei Gonchar and while surrounded by a loud mass of rabid fans at Verizon Center.

"Just, with everything we've gone through, this is who we are," Crosby said last night after fellow star center Evgeni Malkin's sixth playoff goal with a second remaining on an overtime power play pushed the Penguins within a win of a second consecutive berth in the Eastern Conference final.

Malkin's pass attempt to Crosby deflected off Capitals defenseman Tom Poti's stick and past rookie goalie Simeon Varlamov at 3:28 of overtime to give the Penguins a 4-3 victory and 3-2 lead in this best-of-7 series.

The Penguins can clinch the series Monday with a Game 6 victory at Mellon Arena.

Capitals left wing Alex Ovechkin pledged last night to push for a deciding Game 7 on Wednesday in Washington.

"If we play the same way we played in the first two periods," he said, "we're going to win this series."

The Penguins' **Matt Cooke** celebrates his goal with Jordan Staal and Tyler Kennedy during the third period against Washington in Game 5 of the Eastern Conference semifinals.

This series — pitting arguably the NHL's top three young players in Crosby, Malkin and Ovechkin — has proven again that playoff hockey contains no certainties. (Though, the Penguins are now 8-0 in playoff Game 5s against the Capitals.)

These Penguins are certain there is no limit to the number of punches they can take, and confident they will land the final blow.

"We have good players," Malkin said, "and we're tough."

Left wing Matt Cooke, whose first playoff goal at 6:27 of the third period gave the Penguins a 3-2 lead, said he noticed that toughness a year ago as he watched the nucleus of this club come within two victories of the Stanley Cup.

"Obviously, there were a lot of personnel changes," Cooke said of the Penguins losing six forwards from that 2008 final roster last summer and former coach Michel Therrien, who was fired Feb. 15 with this team mired 10th in the East and five points from a playoff spot.

"They handled themselves very well in the playoffs last year, and it's the reason I had interest in coming to Pittsburgh."

Center Jordan Staal came to Pittsburgh as an 18-year-old in June 2006 as the second-overall draft choice. Now 20, Staal snapped a 16-game playoff goal drought at 5:17 of the second period last night to give the Penguins a 1-0 lead.

Ovechkin, a terror this series with seven goals, needed only 59 seconds to respond. His tally at 6:16 tied the score, 1-1.

A power-play goal by Capitals center Nicklas Backstrom pushed them ahead, 2-1, at 14:35. The Penguins had been penalized for having too many players on the ice.

Washington was undefeated in the playoffs when leading after any period, but its lead was short-lived in the third. Penguins left wing Ruslan Fedotenko scored his third goal in as many games — only 51 seconds in — and the score was again tied, 2-2.

Cooke's goal about six minutes later gave the Penguins a lead that held until Ovechkin's 10th of the playoffs with 4:08 remaining in regulation forced the second overtime game of the series.

Penguins winger Craig Adams, who joined the club as a waiver-wire acquisition March 4, admitted last night that many teams would have crumbled following Ovechkin's tying goal.

"But I found out pretty quick these guys don't crack when adversity hits," Adams said. "They're young, but they've seen a lot and they know how to handle pressure."

So, it was not a crippling blow that Gonchar, their power-play anchor and a calming presence overall, did not play because of a right-knee injury from Friday's Game 4 at Mellon Arena.

After all, the Penguins had played 57 regular-season games without Gonchar — including their first 56 as he recovered from left-shoulder surgery.

Fittingly, a power-play attack that has absorbed verbal blows from the public and pundits all season, especially in the playoffs, provided the Penguins with a perfect-timing goal in this pivotal Game 5.

"It's not something we talk about a lot or at all, really," Crosby said of his club's resiliency. "It's just something we've developed over the last few years because a lot of us have gone through this together.

"You just expect it of yourself not to give up or give in, and you expect the guy sitting next to you to expect the same. That's what we have on this team. That's us."

CROSBY, PENGUINS CHASE CAPS FROM PLAYOFFS

By Rob Rossi/TRIB TOTAL MEDIA

○ ○ ○ ○ ○

Thursday, May 14, 2009

WASHINGTON — Sidney Crosby's Penguins went on a hunt Wednesday that will leave Alex Ovechkin's Capitals red until October.

Crosby capped a crushing defeat for his archrival with a breakaway goal early in the third period — his second power-play tally of the contest — and the Penguins dominated the Washington Capitals, 6-2, at Verizon Center to win a best-of-7 Stanley Cup playoff second-round series, 4-3.

As a franchise, the Penguins improved to 4-0 all-time in road playoff Game 7s and are 7-1 in postseason series against the Capitals.

These Penguins strolled into their second straight Eastern Conference final — either top-seeded Boston or sixth seed Carolina will be their opponent — with a blowout victory in Game 7 of a series that had produced five one-goal contests and three overtime games.

However, close was not going to cut it for Crosby, the

The Penguins' **Sidney Crosby** scores a power-play goal past Washington goaltender Simeon Varlamov during the first period in Game 7 of the Eastern Conference semifinals.

Christopher Horner/Trib Total Media

The Penguins' **Craig Adams** (right) celebrates his goal with **Max Talbot** and **Ruslan Fedotenko** during the first-period of Game 7 against the Capitals.

The Penguins' **Sergei Gonchar** talks with Washington's Alex Ovechkin after the Penguins' Game 7 victory.

Christopher Horner photos/Trib Total Media

Penguins' captain, last night.

"We got the lead," he said last night, after he scored the Penguins' first goal, a power-play tally, at 12:36 of the first period.

"So many times throughout the first six (games) we got a lead and it was only a one-goal lead, and we allowed, basically, one mistake to let them back in the hockey game."

That script did not hold in Game 7, and the Penguins chased previously unflappable Capitals rookie goalie Simeon Varlamov less than 23 minutes into the contest by scoring on four of 18 shots.

Gritty winger Craig Adams' first career playoff goal only eight seconds after Crosby's opening score gave the Penguins a 2-0 lead. That time between goals is the second shortest in franchise playoff history behind seven seconds that separated goals by Ron Stackhouse and Rick Kehoe on April 13, 1980.

The Penguins opened the second period last night with right wing Bill Guerin's fifth playoff goal just 28 seconds in, and defenseman Kris Letang's third goal of the series at 2:12 forced Washington coach Bruce Boudreau to yank Varlamov, who had recorded a .907 save percentage in six previous series contests.

"After the third goal I was thinking of pulling him because he looked really dejected, and maybe I should have called a timeout at that point," Boudreau said. "I think after that fourth goal the wind completely came out of his sails emotionally."

Former starter Jose Theodore replaced Varlamov and allowed Penguins center Jordan Staal's second playoff goal at 11:37. The Penguins were up, 5-0.

Ovechkin tallied for the Capitals at 18:09 of the second to bring his club within 5-1. Forward Brooks Laich tallied his third playoff goal at 6:35 of the third period, but the outcome had long since been decided.

Crosby decided early in this series that he would make quarters around the goal crease his personal property. All but the first and last of his six series goals at Washington were scored by trolling around the blue paint.

His much-anticipated duel with Ovechkin — they are the last two league MVPs — surpassed expectations. Ovechkin won the individual duel with eight goals and 14 points.

However, Crosby's club experienced a victorious post-series handshake, and his eight goals and 13 points proved that he and Ovechkin stand together as the sport's top young stars.

"Maybe it's 1-A and 1-B, but going into Game 7, he's the guy you want on your team," defenseman Brooks Orpik said.

"All three are great players, and we're lucky enough to have two of them on our team."

Penguins center Evgeni Malkin, the NHL's regular-season scoring leader, recorded two assists last night to finish the series with two goals and 10 points.

Malkin deflected praise to Crosby last night.

"He played great," he said. "We followed his lead the whole game."

The Penguins' **Evgeni Malkin** celebrates his second goal in the third-period of Game 2 of the Eastern Conference final at Mellon Arena.

MALKIN'S HAT TRICK PUTS PENS IN CONTROL

By Rob Rossi/TRIB TOTAL MEDIA

○ ○ ○ ○ ○

Friday, May 22, 2009

They're not quite magnificent yet, but Penguins centers Evgeni Malkin and Sidney Crosby have impressed at least one NHL legend with their Stanley Cup playoff performances.

"Pretty good, huh?" Hall-of-Fame player and Penguins co-owner Mario Lemieux said Thursday after Malkin (three goals, four points) and Crosby (a goal and an assist) helped deliver the Penguins a 7-4 victory over the Carolina Hurricanes at Mellon Arena and a 2-0 lead in the best-of-7 Eastern Conference Final.

Everybody inside the league's oldest building last night watched Malkin perform at a level that Penguins defenseman Philippe Boucher said was comparable to all-time scoring leader Wayne Gretzky.

"I played with him (in 1994), the year after they went to the (Stanley Cup Final)," Boucher said of Gretzky. "He was the one guy that I played with that could just do whatever he wanted.

"It's tough here, though, because we've got two."

Last night, Malkin's ninth and 10th playoff goals — at 8:50 and 12:25 of the third period — snapped a 4-4 tie, and winger Tyler Kennedy's empty-net third playoff tally cinched a sweep of opening home games in the series, which continues Saturday at Carolina's RBC Center.

"It's my job," said Malkin, who has scored five goals and recorded 13 points over a five-game scoring streak.

"I try to win every game."

He and Crosby are pushing the Penguins in that direction. They are 6-1 since dropping Games 1 and 2 at Washington in a second-round series at Washington against the Capitals.

Malkin's 25 points are tops in the postseason. Crosby, whose 13th goal opened the scoring, is second with 24 points.

"They're hurting us too bad," Hurricanes coach Paul Maurice said of Malkin and Crosby, who have combined to score five goals and record nine points through two series games.

Lemieux, a two-time playoff MVP and the Penguins' all-time scoring leader, compared his "Mega Powers" pivots to famed Boston Bruins duo Phil Esposito and Bobby Orr, who traded regular-season scoring titles in the late-1960s and early-1970s and won the Cup twice over that span.

Penguins defenseman Sergei Gonchar said "nothing needs to be said" about Malkin and Crosby, but later compared their playoff dominance to those by Lemieux and former Penguins winger Jaromir Jagr in the 1990s.

"That's the closest I can think of," Penguins goaltending coach and former NHL goalie Gilles Meloche said. "You don't really realize what you're seeing on a daily basis. They keep amazing all of us."

Crosby and Malkin have won two of the past three points championships, with Malkin claiming his first Art Ross Trophy this season.

His standing as the scoring champion was the basis of criticism sent his way after he went five games without a goal from late in the first to early in the second playoff round.

Malkin insists harsh words from others had no effect on his play, but an exchange of punches with Carolina winger Chad LaRose midway through the second period last night seemed to light his fire.

In fact, Malkin described his first NHL fight with an expletive.

At that point, the score was tied, 3-3.

Penguins center Max Talbot's third playoff goal at 3:11 of the second, Crosby's record-tying sixth opening goal at 1:51 of the first along with Malkin's at 8:15 had equaled three opening-period scores by the Hurricanes. La Rose scored his fourth at 3:07, forward Jussi Jokinen his seventh at 8:40 and defenseman Dennis Seidenberg his first at 12:10.

"More goals than I would have liked," Penguins goalie Marc-Andre Fleury said after stopping 24 shots in the contest. "So, it was nice to see the team come back."

Winger Chris Kunitz snapped a 19-game goal drought with his first playoff tally since May 11, 2007 — as a member of the Stanley Cup champion Anaheim Ducks.

Kunitz, who added two assists, scored with eight seconds remaining in the second period, and the Penguins led, 4-3.

Carolina forward Patrick Eaves' first playoff goal at 2:35 of the third period tied the score, 4-4 and soon after, as Talbot said, "Geno just took over."

Malkin put the Penguins ahead, 5-4, at 8:50, but the backhand shot he placed behind Hurricanes goalie Cam Ward at 12:25 was eye-popping.

"It's a faceoff play. It's called the 'Geno' for a reason," Penguins coach Dan Bylsma said. "He pushed (the puck) through, got it himself. After that, it's all him.

"He takes it to the net, spins on his backhand. There's not a lot of room where he put it. There's not a lot of players in the world that can make a play like that — two of them are on our team."

The Penguins' **Evgeni Malkin** scores the game-winning goal on Carolina goaltender Cam Ward during the third period in Game 2 of the Eastern Conference final.

Christopher Horner/Trib Total Media

PENGUINS EARN ANOTHER SHOT AT LORD STANLEY

By Rob Rossi/TRIB TOTAL MEDIA

○ ○ ○ ○ ○

Wednesday, May 27, 2009

RALEIGH, N.C. — Stunned?

"No, I wouldn't say so," Penguins winger Craig Adams said Tuesday night after his empty-net goal flipped the electrocution switch on his former team, the Carolina Hurricanes, in the Eastern Conference final.

"I've been in that situation. You go to the Stanley Cup Final ... and the next year you struggle because you forget what it takes to win."

The Penguins have remembered.

With their 30th win in 42 games under coach Dan Bylsma, the Penguins are again bound for the Stanley Cup Final. They wrapped up a convincing four-game sweep of the Hurricanes with a 4-1 victory at RBC Center.

Not lost in the details of this win — goalie Marc-Andre Fleury's 30 saves and wingers Ruslan Fedotenko, Max Talbot, Bill Guerin and Adams answering an opening goal by Carolina center Eric Staal — was what it means.

"We have another opportunity," Penguins center and captain Sidney Crosby said of the chance to return the Cup to Pittsburgh for a third time.

By winning for the eighth time in nine games to claim this best-of-7 series, 4-0, the Penguins became the first

Penguins captain **Sidney Crosby** holds the Prince of Wales Trophy with NHL deputy commissioner Bill Daly after the Penguins beat the Carolina Hurricanes for the Eastern Conference title at the RBC Center.

(Left) Penguins goaltender **Marc-Andre Fleury** stops a shot by Carolina's Eric Staal during the third period in Game 4 of the Eastern Conference Final at RBC Center in Raleigh, N.C.

(Right) The Penguins' **Sidney Crosby** celebrates winning the Eastern Conference with **Mario Lemieux** after beating the Hurricanes.

Christopher Horner/Trib Total Media

Chaz Palla/Trib Total Media

NHL team since the 1984 Edmonton Oilers to reach the Cup final after losing in it the previous season.

If the defending champion Detroit Red Wings beat the Chicago Blackhawks at home tonight to end their Western Conference final series, a Cup final rematch — the likelihood of which Penguins center Jordan Staal admitted last night seemed bleak just three months ago — will likely open this weekend with Games 1 and 2 at Joe Louis Arena.

Few Penguins players would admit to craving another shot at the Red Wings, who raised the Cup on Mellon Arena ice last season.

However, as center Max Talbot said last night from a dressing room full with satisfied — though hardly content — teammates, "We're back, and we'll be ready for whoever we play."

Hurricanes winger Scott Walker sensed determination from the Penguins in a series in which they outscored Carolina, 20-9.

"You can tell they were there last year and they want a chance to do it again," he said. "I wouldn't really want to be facing them if I'm one of the other two teams. They're playing at a real high level right now. I think that year experience has definitely given them a lot of confidence."

Besting the modern-day dynastic Red Wings — four Cup titles since 1997 — or the burgeoning-power Blackhawks may prove no greater challenge to these Penguins than did qualifying for the Stanley Cup playoffs.

Fleury described his club's regular season as having "some ups and downs."

At one point, retirement savings appeared more stable than the Penguins' playoff chances.

They were 10th in the East, five points from the final playoff spot, when coach Bylsma — coaching in the American Hockey League when the season began — replaced Michel Therrien on Feb. 15.

Bylsma, then on an interim basis, instituted an up-tempo style to make better use of skill possessed by Crosby; would-be league scoring champion Evgeni Malkin; and puck-moving defensemen Sergei Gonchar, who had recently returned from a 56-game absence because of a left-shoulder injury, and Kris Letang.

He also steered the Penguins on an improbable 18-3-4 march that gave them home-ice advantage in the first playoff round, and a No. 4 seed that afforded them the same advantage in this series against sixth-seed Carolina.

A couple of acquisitions by general manager Ray Shero on March 4 — veteran wingers Guerin and Adams, who have combined for 10 playoff goals — and the Penguins, Staal said, "felt like a different team."

Or, as Talbot put it, "like ourselves again."

They opened the playoffs with a tough six-game victory against Philadelphia and outlasted reigning league MVP Alex Ovechkin's Washington club in seven second-round games.

The Hurricanes have many players from a team that won the Cup in 2006, including goalie Cam Ward, who was undefeated in six playoff series.

But they never really had a chance.

"We've got a pretty special group of guys here," Guerin said.

That group senses a special opportunity to makes itself immortal in this sport's history.

"We feel like this group in this dressing room still has a lot to prove yet," winger Matt Cooke said. "Yeah, we're back in the Stanley Cup Final, but we're not done.

"We have a lot to accomplish yet."

The Red Wings' Brad Stuart defends against the Penguins' **Evgeni Malkin** in the third period of Game 1 of the Stanley Cup Final at Joe Louis Arena.

PENGUINS NEED TO CIRCLE THE WAGONS, AGAIN

By Rob Rossi/TRIB TOTAL MEDIA

○ ○ ○ ○ ○

Sunday, May 31, 2009

DETROIT — Face it, the Penguins need to win some faceoffs, or they'll face another deep hole in the Stanley Cup Final.

A sorry 16-of-55 performance in the faceoff circle Saturday — including just two wins in the third period — and some bad-luck goals doomed the Penguins in a 3-1 Game 1 loss to the Detroit Red Wings at Joe Louis Arena.

Like last season, they trail the best-of-7 Final, 1-0. However, as forward Max Talbot said last night, "the goal when you start on the road is to win one of two."

The Penguins have that opportunity tonight. Game 2 is at 8 p.m, and they're still the team with younger legs and fewer injuries.

They also have a defiant sense of confidence despite this loss.

"Definitely," center Sidney Crosby said of liking his club's chance to win the Cup more now than at this point last season.

The Penguins were blanked in Game 1 — and later Game 2 — to begin the 2008 Final in Detroit.

They carried the play to the Red Wings more last

night than the combined six Final games last season.

The Penguins out-shot Detroit last night, 32-30, but their advantage in scoring chances appeared more significant. They also won the battle of blocked shots (14-11), giveaways (13-20) and essentially went hit-for-hit (39-43) with the Red Wings.

Penguins coach Dan Bylsma can draw a big circle around what his club did in the those big red circles on the ice.

"They're a puck-possession team, as are we," he said. "And starting with the puck is better than not.

"One of the things we've talked about is our wingers being aware and ready to jump in and help out. The (center) doesn't often win it clean back. A lot of those (Red Wings' faceoff wins) are puck battles off the draw. Being aware, being ready and winning those battles are the responsibility of the wingers and the (defensemen) in the defensive zone.

"So, that's an area we can do a better job of."

Some frightening faceoff statistics from last night: Crosby, 6 of 20; Evgeni Malkin, 4 of 9; Talbot, 0 of 4; and Jordan Staal, 6 of 19.

Red Wings coach Mike Babcock did not see those performances as the start of a series trend.

"Just a night," he said. "I think it goes that way. Some nights it goes your way, other nights it doesn't."

It went against Penguins goalie Marc-Andre Fleury last night.

Detroit went ahead, 1-0, at 13:38 of the first period on defenseman Brad Stuart's second playoff goal. His point-shot ricocheted off the backboards, slid toward Fleury, under his leg pads and over the goal line.

Malkin and winger Ruslan Fedotenko provided the Penguins with a counterpunch.

Malkin intercepted a clear-attempt by Stuart in the offensive zone and fired quickly on Red Wings goalie Chris Osgood. Fedotenko skated into the slot and stuffed a rebound into the net for his seventh playoff goal to tie the score, 1-1.

The Penguins owned the second period more than their 13-11 shots advantage suggested.

Osgood, though, showed the poise of a two-time Cup-winning starter. He denied Malkin on an early-period breakaway and later prevented Crosby from a highlight-reel finish to a spinning-backhand shot. Also, winger Miroslav Satan could not control a puck near the crease with much of the net open.

"We found a way to generate some good scoring opportunities," Crosby said. "Certainly if we would have buried a couple there we would have put ourselves in a better position."

Detroit jumped ahead, 2-1, with 58 seconds left in the second on winger Johan Franzen's 11th playoff goal.

Out of a Penguins' timeout called by Bylsma to rest exhausted players following an icing of the puck, Crosby lost a faceoff to Henrik Zetterberg. A couple of weird bounces later — one, again, off the backboards — Franzen was credited with a goal off a shot that was really a behind-the-back pass toward the slot to winger Dan Cleary.

Winger Justin Abdelkader's first career playoff score at 2:46 of the third period came off another fortunate bounce. He settled a rebound off his own shot and whipped a puck past Fleury to give the Red Wings a two-goal cushion.

"You just can't give them any freebies," Orpik said. "Any mistakes you make, they capitalize, and that's usually the difference in the game.

"But this feels a lot different than last year."

The Red Wings celebrate Brad Stuart's goal during the first period in Game 1 of the Stanley Cup Final against the Penguins.

STANLEY CUP IS HALF-EMPTY FOR PENGUINS

By Rob Rossi/TRIB TOTAL MEDIA

○ ○ ○ ○ ○

Monday, June 1, 2009

DETROIT — As Penguins captain Sidney Crosby sat Sunday night in his dressing-room stall, without a point through two losing games of a Stanley Cup Final, someone suggested that his team would not only climb out of another 2-0 series hole but rebound to win the Cup.

"I like it," he said.

He's not the only one.

Whether it was collective blind faith or steel-willed belief, Penguins players echoed veteran defenseman Sergei Gonchar's statement following a 3-1 loss to the Detroit Red Wings in Game 2 at Joe Louis Arena.

"We have a good chance," Gonchar said of winning this best-of-7 series. "There are not a lot of teams that can come here and outshoot the Detroit Red Wings (in consecutive games). We've had a lot of chances."

But the Penguins aren't scoring — and the only one who did, center Evgeni Malkin, wasn't talking about how his club might be able to beat red-hot Red Wings goalie Chris Osgood, who made 31 saves for a second consecutive game.

Actually, Malkin refused to speak after a game that for him ended with 19 seconds remaining because of a seemingly frustration-fueled fight with Red Wings center Henrik Zetterberg.

So, there is no way to know if Malkin was sending a message to the Red Wings in advance of Game 3 at Mellon Arena on Tuesday.

Only one team in NHL history — the 1971 Montreal Canadiens — has won a best-of-7 Final after losing two opening games on the road.

Home will certainly seem comforting to the Penguins.

Unlike last year, when they failed to score in Games 1 and 2 at Detroit, they've gone shift-for-shift with the Red Wings in this Final.

However, suspect non-calls, off-the-mark bounces and weird goals went against them.

Penguins goaltender **Marc-Andre Fleury** can't stop the Red Wings' third goal during the third period of Game 2 of the Stanley Cup Final at Joe Louis Arena in Detroit.

Start backward with the fourth baffling goal surrendered by Marc-Andre Fleury. The Penguins trailed, 2-1, early in the third period when Red Wings winger Justin Abdelkader's second series goal somehow eluded Fleury. After cutting across the ice in the offensive zone against Penguins defensemen Hal Gill and Rob Scuderi, Abdelkader whacked a bouncing puck high past Fleury's glove hand.

"In the playoffs, it's up to the goalie to play well and make those key saves for your team," Fleury said. "I have to do that more in the next (game)."

Fleury has allowed six goals on 56 shots for a .892 save percentage that he knows won't cut it against the high-powered Red Wings, even if few of Detroit's offensive stars have bested him in the Final.

Crosby, the Penguins' top star and captain, has yet to make his mark.

Accused yesterday morning by Detroit coach Mike Babcock of being a headhunter for a Game 1 check on Zetterberg, Crosby was determined to deliver in Game 2.

To be fair, he could have had his 15th playoff goal and an assist, but he hit the post shortly before Abdelkader's goal, as did Penguins right wing Bill Guerin not long after Red Wings center Valtteri Filppula's winning goal at 10:29 of the second period.

That goal enraged the Penguins, who feel former teammate and Red Wings winger Marian Hossa should have been penalized for hooking winger Pascal Dupuis.

As Dupuis skated with the puck high in the defensive zone, Hossa lifted his stick into Dupuis' gloves to force a turnover. Dupuis said his stick was broken by Hossa, and he looked to officials for a call.

By then, Detroit winger Tomas Holmstrom had directed a shot on Fleury, whose crease was crowded by Red Wings and Penguins. Filppula found the rebound and directed the puck into the net to give the Red Wings a 2-1 lead.

"He hooks me in the hands and breaks my stick, and there was no explanation (from on-ice officials) on that," Dupuis said. "I thought maybe there should have been a call on that play. It's frustrating."

Equally frustrating was Detroit pulling even at 4:21 of the second period on defenseman Jonathan Ericsson's third playoff goal — a point-shot that beat Fleury, who was cleanly screened by Red Wings center Darren Helm.

That goal — like Red Wings winger Johan Franzen's winner late in the second period of Game 1 on Saturday — was set up by a Penguins faceoff loss following an icing on an extended shift.

It was one of those weekends for the Penguins, but ...

"I think everybody in this room believes we have a great, great chance of winning this series," winger Chris Kunitz said. "I think we've played well. Obviously, they've played better. They've got the two wins. But we still believe we have a great, great chance."

Pens drop Game 2, head home for uphill climb

The Penguins' **Evgeni Malkin** grimaces on the bench during the second period of Game 2.

The Penguins' **Sidney Crosby** celebrates a goal as Red Wings goalie Chris Osgood reacts during the third period of Game 3 of the Stanley Cup Final at Mellon Arena.

PENGUINS BEAT RED WINGS, 4-2, IN GAME 3 OF CUP FINAL

By Rob Rossi/TRIB TOTAL MEDIA

○ ○ ○ ○ ○

Wednesday, June 3, 2009

These gut-check victories, it's all they ever have.

With their Stanley Cup dreams in the balance Tuesday, redemption performances by goalie Marc-Andre Fleury (27 saves) and forward Max Talbot (two goals) pushed the Penguins past the Detroit Red Wings, 4-2, at Mellon Arena in Game 3 of the Stanley Cup Final.

"It feels great," Talbot said after his fifth and sixth playoff goals opened and closed the scoring last night. "It was a big win. I don't want to say it was must-win, but everybody knows it was."

The Penguins trail the best-of-7 Final, 2-1, but can pull even Thursday with another home victory.

This scenario mirrors the 2008 Final, which the Penguins lost in six games after also dropping Games 1 and 2 at Detroit and responding with a Game 3 home victory.

Of course, the Red Wings won Game 4 in that Final to tilt the series for good.

Aside from dealing with the Penguins' collective never-wilt spirit — the Red Wings have a real reason to be concerned.

Penguins center Evgeni Malkin appears to be taking over the hockey world.

He recorded primary assists on three goals last night,

giving him a goal and five points in the series. He leads all playoff scorers with 33 points.

"He's found an ability to elevate his game to another level," said defenseman Sergei Gonchar, whose slap-shot blast on a power-play midway through the third period snapped a 2-2 tie. "He was good all over the ice, not only offensively but defensively — blocking a shot at the end — and doing some great things for the team.

"It seems like he's improving and maturing as a player."

This victory shows that the Penguins are improving and maturing as a Cup contender, and Fleury and Talbot are the front line of that charge.

Though teammates such as defenseman Brooks Orpik defended his weekend performances at Detroit, Fleury allowed six goals on 56 shots, a poor .893 save percentage. Four of the goals he surrendered could kindly be described as baffling — a few weird bounces off the Joe Louis Arena boards not withstanding.

Last night, Fleury played like a true shut-down goalie. His 14 saves in the second period, when many Penguins players admit they were "off their game," impressed Red Wings coach Mike Babcock.

"I thought they played a good first 10 minutes," he said. "I thought we took the game over for about the next 30 minutes and really had great opportunities in the second (period) — probably as many as we've had at any period of time.

"We didn't score."

Detroit also failed to generate anything early in the third period, and finished it with only three shots — setting the stage for Gonchar's winning power-play tally at 10:29, his third of the playoffs, and Talbot's empty-net clincher.

Talbot lost a defensive-zone faceoff Sunday in Game 2 that led directly to Detroit defenseman Jonathan Ericsson's tying-tally, so he was considerably pleased to whip a one-timer past Detroit goalie Chris Osgood (17 saves) at 4:48 of the first period last night.

That goal put the Penguins ahead, 1-0, but the Red Wings responded with goals by star forwards Henrik Zetterberg and Johan Franzen. Zetterberg netted his 10th at 6:19, and Franzen scored his 12th at 11:33 to give the Red Wings a 2-1 lead.

A sellout crowd was noticeably silent, but fans sprung to life on Penguins defenseman Kris Letang's slap-shot goal, his fourth, on the power play at 15:57.

The Penguins went 2-for-3 on the power play and have scored three of their five goals in the series with the advantage.

Malkin recorded primary assists on all but Talbot's empty-net goal, and Fleury was super sharp when it mattered most, as his goalie coach figured would be the case.

"I saw him in the morning and he didn't have to say much because he was smiling," Gilles Meloche said. "With Marc-Andre, that's all you need to see. That smile means he's about to make a difference for us.

"He did."

A crowd of thousands gathers outside Mellon Arena to watch Game 3 of the Stanley Cup Final on the Trib Tron.

PENS MAKE STANLEY CUP FINAL INTO A BEST-OF-THREE

By Rob Rossi/TRIB TOTAL MEDIA

○ ○ ○ ○ ○

Friday, June 5, 2009

Hey, Hockeytown, get your motor running because the Penguins are even and believin'.

"We wanted to make a statement, and (we) want to continue to make a statement," defenseman Hal Gill said after the Penguins' 4-2 victory Thursday over the Detroit Red Wings at Mellon Arena, which tied the best-of-7 Stanley Cup Final series, 2-2. "Not to anybody else, but to ourselves."

Game 5 is Saturday at Detroit's Joe Louis Arena, and the defending Cup-champion Red Wings can sleep on this ...

"We can beat these guys," Gill said. "We found that confidence."

They did so exactly one year to the night they watched the Red Wings raise the Cup on their home ice.

Last night, the Penguins won the Game 4 at home that they lost last year to swing that Final in the Red Wings' favor.

Now, as defenseman Brooks Orpik said last night, "maybe we swung momentum on our side."

Enough from the Penguins' defensemen, though.

This one belonged to their "Big Three," and a guy that soon could make that a "Fantastic Four."

Centers Evgeni Malkin, Sidney Crosby and Jordan Staal combined for three goals and six points, and goalie Marc-Andre Fleury turned aside 37 shots — including 18 in a first period the Penguins thought they had won, only to finish it tied.

Malkin's 14th goal on a power play gave them a 1-0 lead at 2:39, but that edge evaporated late in the first period. Defenseman Rob Scuderi's deep defensive-zone turnover was intercepted by Red Wings center Darren Helm, who beat Fleury with 1:41 remaining to pull Detroit even, 1-1.

That staggering blow was followed by what felt like a dead-to-rights punch by Red Wings defenseman Brad Stuart, whose second Final goal 46 seconds into the second period pushed Detroit to a 2-1 lead.

Bad became worse for the Penguins.

Malkin was penalized for hooking in the offensive zone at 5:44, and the Penguins were two seconds from killing the Red Wings' power-play chance when Orpik was sent to the box for tripping behind the cage in the defensive zone at 7:43.

A two-second 5-on-3 advantage nearly turned disastrous for Detroit, though, as Malkin stepped out of the box, won possession of the puck and broke into the offensive zone on Red Wings goalie Chris Osgood. However, Malkin was chased by rugged Red Wings winger Johan Franzen, who bumped him from the puck before he could get off a shot.

At that point, Malkin's failure to get a tying goal seemed like just another missed chance for the Penguins, who could not convert on several first-period chances to gain a two-goal cushion.

Plus, they still had to kill a power play.

Turns out, the Red Wings were about to be killed on their advantage.

Staal, whose first-period effort was impressive, turned Game 4 around with a shorthanded goal — his first in 10 career Final games — at 8:35.

Taking a page from his rookie yearbook, Staal, who had seven shorthanded goals that season, darted into the offensive zone, swept around Red Wings defenseman Brian Rafalski and went backhand-to-forehand to send a shot past Osgood and tie the score, 2-2.

"Our power play sucked the life out of us tonight," Red Wings coach Mike Babcock said of a power-play attack that went 0-for-4 and is 1-for-10 in the Final.

The Penguins, conversely, are 4-for-9 on the advantage after a 1-for-3 performance last night.

Just under two minutes after Staal's goal, Crosby tallied his first goal of the Final and playoff-leading 15th at 10:34. He finished a 2-on-1 with Malkin.

The Penguins' **Evgeni Malkin** scores on Detroit goaltender Chris Osgood during the first period in Game 4 of the Stanley Cup Final at Mellon Arena.

"One of the strengths of our teams is to have those three guys down the middle," Penguins coach Dan Bylsma said of Malkin, Crosby and Staal.

Malkin is making a case — though not verbally, as he did not speak for more than an hour after Game 4 — for playoff MVP. He leads the postseason with 35 points, including seven in the Final.

That is a drastic improvement from last season, when Malkin recorded only three points in six Stanley Cup Final games.

The Penguins finished their second-period surge with a tic-tac-toe goal — winger Chris Kunitz to Crosby to winger Tyler Kennedy — at 14:12 that gave the Penguins a 4-2 lead. Kennedy's first career Final goal was his fourth of the postseason, and all he had to do was ping a puck into an open net.

Osgood was left for dead by the Penguins' pinpoint passing on the sequence.

The Red Wings charged hard in the final period. They outshot the Penguins, 11-9, but Fleury was again strong, stopping every shot.

After allowing six goals on 56 shots in Games 1 and 2 at Detroit, Fleury turned aside 64 of 68 shots in two wins at home.

"I'll try to stop pucks and there will be some tough nights," Fleury said. "But the most important thing is to forget about it as quick as possible and start over again in the next one."

THE GENOS

MALKIN'S PARENTS SCORE BIG IN CITY THAT LOVES SON

By Rob Rossi/TRIB TOTAL MEDIA

○ ○ ○ ○ ○

Sunday, April 19, 2009

He has transformed from a Stanley Cup Final flameout to Conn Smythe Trophy favorite in just a year, but the Malkin Pittsburghers dig most isn't named Evgeni.

The Penguins star's parents — Vladimir, 51, and Natalia, 49, known lovingly by locals as "The Genos" — have become Pittsburgh's unofficial first couple over the past two months.

"Interviews, pictures, autographs ... (people) ask us to sign anything," Vladimir Malkin said Friday through family friend and unofficial Penguins Russian translator George Birman. "We'd like to stay out of the spotlight, but how can you say no when people ask for your autograph or want to take a picture?

"I had one young girl ask me to kiss her. (My son) doesn't know."

A sit-down interview with Evgeni Malkin's parents, who do not speak English, revealed them as free spirits who laugh at their own jokes and are enjoying their son's on-ice success and their off-ice popularity.

"When he was 17 he started to play on so many (traveling) teams that we didn't see him a lot, probably less than most parents see their children at that time," Vladimir Malkin said of Evgeni, 22. "We've not had this period where it's so much us being parents looking over him."

So, Natalia Malkin interjected, "We come here, and he's like the parents to us because he knows what's best in Pittsburgh."

Evgeni Malkin did not comment for this story. After an optional practice for the Penguins at Mellon Arena, he quickly left the facility and drove to his home in Sewickley — to say goodbye to them, his parents said, before driving off to catch a charter plane to Detroit.

Tonight he will try to fan the flames of his hot Stanley Cup Final in a pivotal Game 5 between the Penguins and Red Wings at Joe Louis Arena. The best-of-7 series is tied, 2-2, and Malkin leads all players with seven points.

Malkin is the playoff leader with 35 points — the most by any player since 1993. His 14 goals are second only to teammate Sidney Crosby. He is trekking toward legendary company. Only Hall-of-Famers Wayne Gretzky and former Penguins star Mario Lemieux have recorded at least 40 points in a single playoff season.

THE GENOS

Vladimir Malkin said he is proud but not surprised to see his son quiet critics who labeled him a playoff underachiever after he recorded only three points in a six-game Cup final loss to the Red Wings last season.

"This year, probably because he knows exactly what to expect, he's grown up more, he's more mature. That's why he's playing the way he's playing," he said.

Penguins defenseman Sergei Gonchar believes there is more to his teammate's dominance than what his parents let on.

"With Geno it's very emotional, and seeing him play has meaning for (his parents), so it gives him an extra energy and pushes him a little extra," said Gonchar, a fellow Russian with whom Malkin lived his first two seasons.

"But it also helps that when he goes home they're probably not talking about hockey, and he can get away from what everybody says."

Malkin's parents, said his friend and Pens TV host Alyonka Larionov, are not stereotypically Russian. She thinks that is why fans gravitated toward them at Mellon Arena and on road trips to Washington and Detroit, and the reason Evgeni appears relaxed during this playoff run.

"Typical Russian parents are very strict. You choose a career as a kid, and there are no alternatives, and if you don't put in hard work, you're a failure; that's how my parents were raised and how I was raised," said Larionov, the daughter of Hall of Fame center Igor Larionov.

"The difference with Geno's parents is that they're just loving and supportive, and they let him go do his own thing."

On this trip to Pittsburgh, which Vladimir Malkin said probably would be their last "for at least a year," the Malkins have done their own thing, too.

Since arriving in late February, Natalia Malkin has cooked several meals for her son and teammates including Gonchar and Petr Sykora.

"One night, Petr was eating a big salad, and he said, 'I go to restaurants and pay, but I should just pay you because it's better,' " she said. "Evgeni has told teammates that I like to cook, but maybe he doesn't want them eating all of the food I cook for him."

Like any mother, Natalia rearranged the kitchen of her son's house. Like any father, Vladimir leads the discussions at dinner.

A retired Russian steelworker, Vladimir said parts of the Pittsburgh area ("Aliquippa, a lot") remind him of home, Magnitogorsk. On bus trips to playoff games in Washington and Detroit, he talked about wanting to fish some of the waters he spied through the window.

"George has told everybody that, and now that is all people think I like to do — fish," he joked about Birman, who translated for Evgeni during post-game interviews the last two seasons. "We need to find something else to say about me."

OK, then, there's this:

"I've never seen anything like the reaction people have to them," longtime Pirates media relations director Jim Trdinich said of Malkin's parents.

Trdinich and his brother watched Game 4 of the Cup Final on Thursday from Mellon Arena in section B3, where the Malkins have watched Penguins home playoff games — Vladimir on the edge of his seat, Natalia with her hands folded on her lap.

"Within five minutes everybody was coming up to them, taking pictures with them, slapping high-fives with them," Trdinich said. "It's almost like people in the arena were looking for them."

If so, NHL Network analyst Gary Green has a suggestion for what fans of "The Genos" can say during Game 6 on Tuesday.

"Just say, 'Yellow blue bus,' " he said. "That's how it sounds to a Russian when they say, 'I love you.' "

With its warm reception to them, the Malkins agree that Pittsburgh already has showered them with love.

Vladimir and **Natalia Malkin** celebrate Evgeni's goal during the first period in Game 4 of the Stanley Cup Final.

Christopher Horner photos/Trib Total Media

The spotlight crosses over **Vladimir and Natalia Malkin** as they cheer on the Penguins at the start of Game 4 of the Stanley Cup Final against Detroit at Mellon Arena.

Meet "The Genos"

Outtakes from an English-translation interview with Vladimir and Natalia Malkin, parents of Penguins star Evgeni Malkin:

Q: *How many young ladies in Pittsburgh have told you they are your son's girlfriend?*
NM: A lot.
VM: We don't even know how many, so all we can say is a lot.

Q: *If "The Genos" were a band, who would play what instrument?*
NM: "Geno" would play the drums. That's him, definitely.
VM: I would watch, maybe play piano. She would make the food.
NM: Our other son, Denis, could play guitar.
VM: There is no singer. We're not The Beatles. If somebody at home heard us saying this, they'd never believe it.

Q: *How does Pittsburgh food compare to Russia?*
NM: I think it's good.
VM: It's the same, but we never go out. Everybody here wants her to cook.

Q: *What will people in Pittsburgh do without "The Genos"?*
VM: They'll miss us for a year. Then we'll come back and start all over again with new pictures and more fun.

Red Wings fans cheer behind Penguins center **Evgeni Malkin** after the Red Wings score a second-period power-play goal during Game 5 of the Stanley Cup Final at Joe Louis Arena.

RED WINGS DOMINATE PENS IN GAME 5

By Rob Rossi/TRIB TOTAL MEDIA

○ ○ ○ ○ ○

Sunday, June 7, 2009

DETROIT — They sure went from tired to terrific in a hurry Saturday.

A powerful 5-0 victory over the Penguins at Joe Louis Arena propelled the Detroit Red Wings to within one win of their second consecutive Stanley Cup title.

The Red Wings' three power-play goals in the second period, and one only seconds after an advantage had expired, positioned the Penguins in a familiar spot — a must-win Cup Final Game 6 at Mellon Arena on Tuesday.

Captain Sidney Crosby is confident the Penguins will rebound, unlike last year when he watched the Red Wings skate with the Cup on his home ice.

"We've been through a lot of things. Maybe not a big loss like this in the playoffs, but a lot of things that we've had to bounce back from," Crosby said after finishing with a minus-2 rating and only one shot — his fifth of six career Cup Final game at Detroit without a point.

"Don't get me wrong. This isn't an easy loss. But, you know what, a loss is a loss. ... The reality is we have to go home and win one. We owe it to each other to be a lot better."

The Red Wings, labeled Thursday by some Penguins players as "tired" after the second of two consecutive series losses in Pittsburgh, were better in Game 5 because MVP finalist and two-way dynamo center Pavel Datsyuk returned to the Final in grand style.

After missing the first four series games because of a

reportedly broken right foot, Datsyuk assisted on the Red Wings' first and fourth goals.

He and Red Wings center Henrik Zetterberg combined for one goal and four assists. Conversely, Penguins star pivots Evgeni Malkin and Crosby — the top two playoff scorers — were a combined minus-3, with only one shot apiece.

A couple of Red Wings veteran defensemen, captain Nicklas Lidstrom and Brian Rafalski, combined for a goal and three points.

So, all that tired talk ...

"We didn't listen to it," Zetterberg said.

Detroit's players did listen to coach Mike Babcock's critical words of their power-play performance in a Game 4 loss.

Living with a 1-for-10 production on the power play through four Final games, the Red Wings responded by going 3-for-6 last night before failing to score on three chances with the game's outcome clearly determined in the third period.

The Penguins were less disciplined than a 12-week-old puppy.

Six of their 12 penalties were committed before the third period, and all of them proved costly.

"It wasn't very smart on our part, really," defenseman Brooks Orpik said. "You take penalties and they have the power play the whole time, and it's tough to be physical on them."

The Penguins actually owned the opening 10 minutes, dominating offensive-zone time and registering the first three shots. However, they failed to score, and did not generate a shot on a power-play chance 7:16 into the game.

"(We) didn't quite connect and didn't quite create the opportunities because we were looking to pass," Penguins coach Dan Bylsma said.

That Red Wings' rare penalty kill — they'd surrendered four goals on nine shorthanded situations — turned momentum in their favor.

Right wing Dan Cleary, who was no sure bet to play because of a lower-body injury, put the Red Wings ahead, 1-0, at 13:32.

The Penguins finished the first period with a 10-8 shots advantage, but the Red Wings started the second on a power play because of winger Chris Kunitz's goalie interference penalty 21 seconds before the intermission.

Technically, that power-play chance did not result in a goal. However, no sooner had the Penguins killed it with a defensive-zone clear than Red Wings goalie Chris Osgood expertly passed the puck to the far blue line, where winger Marian Hossa cradled it and dished to center Valtteri Filppula.

Neither Penguins defenseman Mark Eaton nor Malkin, diving toward the crease, could stop Filppula from skating in on goalie Marc-Andre Fleury and beating him between the leg pads with a backhand shot to give the Red Wings a 2-0 lead at 1:44.

Defenseman Niklas Kronwall scored at 6:11, Rafalski at 8:26 and Zetterberg at 15:40 — all power-play goals.

Zetterberg's 11th playoff goal chased Fleury, who stopped only 16 shots in 35:40.

Fleury had not been pulled from a playoff game since his first, Game 1 of an opening-round series against the Senators at Ottawa on April 11, 2007 — a span of 46 postseason contests.

Until last night, that 6-3 loss in Ottawa was the most jarring postseason blow absorbed by these Penguins.

They responded with a victory, and are confident they can respond equally Tuesday.

"They won, they did a good job," Fleury said of the Red Wings. "But we've got to play Tuesday and that's all that matters."

The Red Wings' Henrik Zetterberg celebrates Dan Cleary's goal on Penguins goaltender **Marc-Andre Fleury** during the first period in Game 5.

PENS FORCE DECIDING GAME 7 AGAINST WINGS

By Rob Rossi/TRIB TOTAL MEDIA

○ ○ ○ ○ ○

Wednesday, June 10, 2009

One game for the Stanley Cup.

That is the story of this Final after the Penguins' inspired 2-1 victory Tuesday over the Detroit Red Wings at Mellon Arena.

However, the story of Game 6 was the Penguins' third line.

Goals from third-line forwards Jordan Staal and Tyler Kennedy held thanks to clutch saves by goalie Marc-Andre Fleury and anything-goes play in the crease by defenseman Rob Scuderi. The Penguins forced a deciding Game 7 at Detroit on Friday without superstar centers Evgeni Malkin and Sidney Crosby recording a point last night.

"That's the way we play here," Staal said. "It's a team effort every night. That's what good teams do — find ways to win, whether it's your big guys scoring or the third and fourth lines scoring.

"It's big for us."

A win Friday would be bigger. That would return the Cup to Pittsburgh for a third time and the first since 1992.

Penguins majority co-owner Mario Lemieux captained that 1992 Cup club. Yesterday was the 25th anniversary of his selection by the Penguins as the first overall draft pick in 1984.

Fleury was the first overall pick in 2003, and his 25 saves last night — including 13 in the final period — were a defiant response to his performance in Game 5 at Detroit last Saturday, when he was pulled midway through the game after making just 16 saves.

Fleury's right pad stop on a breakaway backhand by Red Wings winger Daniel Cleary with 1:45 remaining topped the save he made on Capitals winger Alex Ovechkin early in a second-round Game 7 victory at Washington.

Not long after that save, Fleury and Scuderi somehow protected a loose puck in the crease as rugged Red Wings winger Johan Franzen attempted to stuff home the tying goal.

"It was just us trying to do whatever (we) can to stop the puck," Scuderi said. "It's kind of weird to understand (Fleury's) broken English, but I'm pretty sure he was saying, 'Move!'

"Once the puck goes there, you have to try and take a man. I'm sure he wanted me to get out of the way, but that was one of those where I had no choice."

Neither did Staal, Kennedy and winger Matt Cooke, really.

Penguins coach Dan Bylsma said after a 5-0 loss in Game 5 that he would try a more defensive approach to the dangerous top-line duo of Detroit centers Henrik Zetterberg and Pavel Datsyuk, who combined for a goal and four points in that contest.

Cooke said he knew upon hearing Bylsma's statement that he, Staal and Kennedy would draw the difficult assignment of defending arguably the top two-way forwards in hockey.

Staal, though, wasn't thinking just defense.

"You know, Jordy thought we should pop in a couple, too," Kennedy said.

Though they dominated the first period, limiting the Red Wings to only three shots, the Penguins failed to score on their 12 attempts.

However, any sense that the Red Wings would open the second period strong faded when Staal scored 51 seconds in to give the Penguins a 1-0 lead.

In the neutral zone, Staal chipped the puck past Red Wings forward Valtteri Filppula, retrieved it and skated into the offensive zone on a 2-on-1 with Cooke.

Red Wings defenseman Jonathan Ericsson was the lone player back and he slid backwards as Staal looked toward Cooke. Staal tried a shot that Ericsson deflected toward Red Wings goalie Chris Osgood, who could not control the rebound.

Staal stayed on-course, gathered the puck and whipped it past Osgood for his fourth playoff goal and second of the Final.

"He rocketed it off my chin (on) the first one and it

Penguins fans celebrate as the team's bench empties after defeating the Red Wings and forcing a Game 7 in the Stanley Cup Final.

must have went right back on his stick," Osgood said. "It just nicked the bottom of my glove."

Staal said he never considered passing to Cooke.

"He hasn't made a pass to me all year in practice on 2-on-1s, and I go with him every day," Cooke said. "I've been screaming at him to shoot all year, and finally he listened."

The Penguins entered the third period with a 24-12 advantage in shots, but their one-goal lead over the resilient Red Wings was tenuous at best.

Kennedy's fifth playoff goal at 5:35 of the third period staked them to a 2-0 lead.

Strong down-low work by wingers Ruslan Fedotenko and Max Talbot set up Kennedy's opportunity near the side of the crease.

"He's got pretty good hands," Osgood said. "I was worried he was going to jam it. He actually tried to and he saw that he had more time and there was nobody there. He kind of stick-handled it out a bit and put it far side.

"It's a nice play by him."

The Red Wings pulled within a goal at 8:01 on veteran center Kris Draper's first of the playoffs. He roofed a rebound off a shot from Ericsson.

However, a couple of superb penalty kills by the Penguins — Staal is their top forward in that department — and the late heroics of Fleury and Scuderi were enough to get the Penguins within a victory of hockey immortality.

"This was a must-win game," Staal said, "and being able to have a hand in it was really special.

"But we've got one more win to get."

The Penguins' **Max Talbot** raises the Stanley Cup at Joe Louis Arena.

PENGUINS MOTOR AWAY WITH STANLEY CUP TITLE

By Rob Rossi/TRIB TOTAL MEDIA

○ ○ ○ ○ ○

Saturday, June 13, 2009

DETROIT — Kids, they grow up so fast.

The young Penguins grew into champions Friday night.

Playing mostly without 21-year-old captain Sidney Crosby, they dethroned the veteran Detroit Red Wings at Joe Louis Arena with a 2-1 victory to claim the Stanley Cup.

After falling into a 2-0 hole in the best-of-7 Final, the Penguins took four of five against the defending champions.

"I didn't know, coming into my first year, how quick we were going to be able to establish ourselves as a solid team in the NHL," said Crosby, the youngest captain in league history to win the Cup. "We proved pretty quickly that we wanted to make an impact as early as we could."

Forward Max Talbot and goalie Marc-Andre Fleury made the most impact last night.

Talbot scored twice, and Fleury stopped 22 shots to help deliver the Cup to Pittsburgh for a third time, and the first since 1992.

Fleury capped a frantic final minute by making a diving stop on Red Wings defenseman Nicklas Lidstrom's shot right before time expired.

"You've got to make those big ones if you want to be a champion," Fleury said. "That was a big one — the biggest of my life."

After the Red Wings pulled within 2-1 late in the third period, Talbot, whose two goals were scored in the second, eased any tension Fleury may have been feeling.

"I told him I still had the winner; do it for me," said Talbot, who then joked about his nickname, "Bad Hands."

Lidstrom's take on Fleury's Cup-saving stop: "The puck squared out to me, and it was either their (defenseman) or their forward came diving out toward me, and the goalie did the same thing. He pulled across, and I think I hit him in the chest."

Crosby's left knee was injured 5:30 into the second period on a collision with Detroit winger Johan Franzen. No penalty was called. Crosby did not return until 10:25 of the final period — and only for a brief stint.

Playing without their captain didn't faze the Penguins, who became the first NHL team since the 1971 Montreal Canadiens to win Game 7 of the last series on the road.

"We've faced more adversity than that," defenseman Rob Scuderi said. "It was tough for Sid, obviously, but we were confident. It wasn't going to faze us.

"We weren't going to be denied."

Not again, anyway.

The Red Wings beat the Penguins in a six-game Final last year.

The Penguins are the first team since the 1984 Edmonton Oilers to win a Final rematch against a team that beat them the previous season.

"This is why I stayed, to play in games like this," defenseman Brooks Orpik said. "I knew we had a team that would win games like this."

Looking back, it is easy to see why Orpik was so confident.

Crosby led all players with 15 playoff goals. Fellow center Evgeni Malkin paced the postseason with 36 points to earn the Conn Smythe Trophy. Fleury closed out four opponents on their home ice.

None of those players is 25. Center Jordan Staal, two goals in the Final, is 20. Kris Letang, arguably the Penguins' best defenseman in the playoffs, is 21.

Talbot is 25.

Talbot led all players with four Final goals and finished the playoffs with eight. He scored 12 in 75 regular-season games.

After a scoreless first period, Talbot tallied early in the second to put the Penguins ahead at 1:13.

Crosby was injured soon after.

As he chased a loose puck in the neutral zone, Crosby was checked by Franzen, who pinned him against the boards.

Penguins defenseman Hal Gill was penalized for holding the stick of Red Wings forward Pavel Datsyuk a couple of minutes after Crosby left the game. The Penguins killed that penalty and soon turned that momentum into a two-goal cushion.

Winger Chris Kunitz chipped a puck past an offensive-zone pinching Brad Stuart near the blue line. Talbot recovered and led a 2-on-1 with winger Tyler Kennedy.

Talbot opted not to pass, and catching Osgood leaning to his right, roofed a shot into the right corner of the net for a 2-0 lead at 10:07.

The Red Wings charged hard after that point, but did not score until defenseman Jonathan Ericsson's blast beat Fleury at 13:53 of the third period.

With just more than two minutes remaining, Red Wings defenseman Nicklas Kronwall hit the crossbar with a hard shot.

However, the Penguins held off a late rally by the Red Wings, who had an extra attacker with Osgood pulled.

"I can't say what I was thinking in that last minute," Orpik said. "I fell on the puck at the end, and there was six seconds left. It was a long six seconds.

"That save (Fleury) made at the end was the best I've ever seen him make."

That's the other thing about kids: They're unpredictable, and sometimes stubborn.

Penguins win Game 7, capture Stanley Cup

PENGUINS FANS PAY PRICE TO WATCH HISTORY

By Kevin Gorman /TRIB TOTAL MEDIA

○ ○ ○ ○ ○

Saturday, June 13, 2009

DETROIT — They paid the asking price to be part of history, traveling from Pittsburgh to watch the Penguins play the Detroit Red Wings on Friday in a game that would decide the Stanley Cup championship.

For one Penguins fan, it was a matter of two words.

"Bucket list," said Brian Pietrandrea, 34, of Brighton Heights, referring to his compilation of things to do before he dies. "How many opportunities are you going to get to see this? I don't think there's a dollar amount somebody could offer me — outside six figures — to get me to sell this."

Pietrandrea and friend Shawn O'Brien, a season-ticket holder from McCandless, were among the throngs of Penguins fans that flocked to the Motor City for Game 7 of the Stanley Cup Final at Joe Louis Arena. They paid $310 each for tickets, and brought homemade signs, including one that read, "You Guessed Wrong, Hossa" — a reference to winger Marian Hossa, who left the Penguins for the Red Wings via free agency last year because he claimed they gave him "the best chance to win the Cup."

Outside the arena, Michele Papakie painted black and

Penguins faithful gather around WTAE reporter Ari Hait as he delivers a live report before Game 7 of the Stanley Cup Final.

gold the face of her 19-year-old son, Derek, after they drove here from Brush Valley, outside Indiana. Holding a homemade "Who Needs Hossa?" sign, Derek reveled in the festive atmosphere along the Detroit River walkway.

They bought tickets for $630 apiece, which left only enough money for Derek to purchase a Sidney Crosby replica jersey. Michele was stuck wearing an old-school Mario Lemieux jersey from the mid-1990s.

"It's 100 percent worth it," Derek Papakie said. "I love it. I've been to a few of the games outside Mellon Arena on the big screen. I loved the atmosphere in Pittsburgh. This is supposedly 'Hockeytown,' so I had to see."

The Papakies had to return home immediately after the game because today is Derek's orientation for his job as an emergency medical technician. While Derek had to shave his 1 1/2-inch-thick playoff beard for the interview, he wasn't about to miss a chance to see the Penguins win the Stanley Cup.

"We brought his uniform, but he'll probably still have his face painted," Michele said.

Kelci Mullen, 20, of Brighton Heights, and Julie Weeber, 21, of Ross, are too young to remember the Penguins' back-to-back Cup titles in 1991 and '92 and joked that they would go if the Penguins forced a Game 7 this year. When the Penguins won Tuesday, the friends spent the next day searching Web sites for tickets before finding a pair for $515 each on Craigslist.com.

"If you're going to go to one game, this is the game to go to," Weeber said. "The last time they won the Cup, I didn't even know what hockey was. It's exciting to see a young team with players who are our age."

Mark Niskach, 29, of Greenfield, cracked the code for Detroit season-ticket holders by visiting a Red Wings' fan site. He was able to buy four tickets for $140 each, and drove in Friday afternoon with his brother, Matt, and friends Mike Horgos of West Mifflin and Greg Erdely of South Park.

"I've never been to a Game 7, and it's going to be an incredible experience," said Mark Niskach.

"That's why I brought them.

"Hopefully, we'll be able to do this every year."

If not, they at least had a chance to check one thing off their bucket list.

Christopher Horner/Trib Total Media

Penguins fan Michele Papakie of Indiana, Pa., paints the face of her son, Derek, outside Joe Louis Arena before Game 7 of the Stanley Cup Final in Detroit.

Fans celebrate with a homemade Stanley Cup on Carson Street in the South Side after the Pens defeated the Red Wings in Detroit on Friday night.

CITY SAVORS TEAM'S THIRD STANLEY CUP TITLE

By Mike Wereschagin/TRIB TOTAL MEDIA

○ ○ ○ ○ ○

Saturday, June 13, 2009

After the last second ticked off the clock at Joe Louis Arena, the crowds spilled onto sidewalks around the city as Pittsburgh screamed for its new champions.

Leaning out of windows above South Side bars, people banged pots and pans together, as the crowd below cheered the Stanley Cup champion Penguins.

Among the crowd that flooded South Side sidewalks, the Foam Finger Guy — born Andrew Austin, 22, of West Deer — prowled East Carson Street, hoisting his faded faux finger to lead chants of "Lets Go Pens!"

A man proclaiming himself too drunk to talk to a reporter held with white-gloved hands a replica Stanley Cup over his head and encouraged passersby to kiss it.

"It feels great. Once (Detroit) made it 2-1 (in the third period), I was definitely nervous, but I knew right away we were going to take it," said Josh Kaninski, 25, of Carrick, standing on the sidewalk outside Finn McCools in the South Side. "It feels fantastic. We're the city of champions."

The Penguins were still skating around the rink with the Stanley Cup when people began pouring out into the streets in the South Side.

Police reported about 400 to 500 people crowded into the intersection of East Carson and 19th streets. A few moments later, police blocked off East Carson from 10th Street to the Birmingham Bridge.

A few small fires were reported on the street in Oakland and the South Side.

Some revelers broke windows in the 1400 block of East Carson Street, and police began clearing the street around 11:30 p.m. Around midnight, police — some on horseback and others on foot with dogs — began making arrests as they ordered the crowd to clear out.

After Max Talbot's second goal, Dave Currink, who was celebrating his 25th birthday bar-hopping with friends and a tray of Penguins birthday cupcakes, stood at the bar at Dee's Cafe in the South Side and screamed, "This is the best birthday ever!"

For some, last night was the last hurrah in a season worth of playoff rituals. Dean Falavolito, 31, of Carnegie, met three friends at the Sports Rock Cafe in the Strip District before almost every home game. Since the Penguins won each Stanley Cup home game, "we figured it was good luck," Falavolito said.

Gina Malkin — a pink, 9-inch-tall stuffed bunny, that dances and plays a Shania Twain tune when owner Tom Dugan squeezes its foot — stood on Dugan's table at Jerome Bettis' Grille 36 on the North Shore.

"She is very much so our good luck charm," said Dugan, 43, of Cincinnati. After Talbot's second goal, Brian Barclay, 35, of Cincinnati danced around the dining room with Gina, as Twain's voice emerged from the bunny singing, "I'm gonna getcha good."

About 30 travelers stranded at Pittsburgh International Airport after a flight to Newark was delayed poached chairs from the deserted food court and gathered outside the T.G.I. Friday's. The restaurant was closed, but staff had left the televisions on over the bar. As Talbot closed in on the second goal, several leaned forward in their chairs, then leapt into the air.

"Our flight has been delayed, but that's all right," said Rebecca Moidel, 25, of Sewickley, clutching a game towel in her fist. "As long as I can watch the game, it's all right."

About 40 neighbors gathered in the Mt. Lebanon driveway of Terry Lynch, who built an 80-inch screen out of drywall onto which he projected the game. A dozen children played street hockey in Lynch's cul-de-sac.

"I just wanted to take it to a new level," Lynch said. "This is another level, a step up from the block party."

A few dozen people quickly gathered at a private area at Pittsburgh International Airport where the team was expected to arrive.

"We're not leaving until they get here," said Joan Cagney from Brookline.

Michele Fegan, 17, from Cranberry said, "If I were in the position to win the Stanley Cup I would want somebody to support me."

Her friend, Bobby Kuzma, 19, from Moon, said he was there "because Max Talbot is a superstar and deserves to be treated as such."

Ken Kroneberg of Hampton was there with his wife, two children, a niece and a nephew. "We're here because we want our kids to experience this."

About 100 fans were on hand when the team arrived at Pittsburgh International Airport at 3:30 a.m.

Team captain Sidney Crosby put the Stanley Cup trophy in the front seat of his SUV to take it home.

Evgeni Malkin put the Conn Smyth trophy, given to the most valuable player in the playoffs, in the front seat of his car as he drove home.

The fans were kept away from the plane but were allowed to gather on a hill to cheer the players as they went past.

— *Staff writer Michael Hasch contributed to this story.*

Let the celebration begin!

Fans celebrate on the corner of Jane and 21st streets in the South Side in the final seconds of Game 7 when the Pens defeated the Red Wings to win the Stanley Cup.

PENGUINS SHARE THEIR MEMORIES OF CUP WIN

By Rob Rossi and Mike Prisuta/TRIB TOTAL MEDIA

Sunday, June 14, 2009

There is only one Stanley Cup, and the Penguins won it Friday with a spirited 2-1 victory over the defending champion Red Wings at Detroit's Joe Louis Arena in a tense Game 7 of the Final.

As they took turns raising the Cup and celebrating with friends and family, several members of the Penguins organization took time to share their euphoric thoughts —

Max Talbot, who scored their only goals in Game 7:

"Like I like to say, every morning I like to wake up and say today's the best day of my life. Well, today is really the best day of my life."

Captain and center Sidney Crosby, on sharing the Cup with Penguins icon, majority co-owner and his landlord, Mario Lemieux:

"That was amazing for me, personally. He's been so great with us for a long time. He's done so much for the team in Pittsburgh. But especially through this run, he was around us a lot. It was really nice to have him be a part of things. After that last loss in Game 5, he was down in the locker room and telling guys to stay with it. He was a real leader for this team, too."

General manager Ray Shero, on his joining late father and former Flyers coach Fred as a Cup-winner:

"'Win today, walk together forever,' I'm going to stick with that one. My dad said that on May 19, 1974, and it is so true. Every single guy, every coach, we're going to forever be linked together, and it's just a wonderful feeling. Every time we see the Cup or go to the Hockey Hall of Fame, my kids look for their (grandfather's) name. And now they'll see their dad's name. It's awesome."

Goalie Marc-Andre Fleury, on silencing his critics:

"You've got to make your name, you know. Mine is going on the Cup."

Coach Dan Bylsma, on winning the Cup four months after he was hired to replace Michel Therrien:

"I haven't won something other than (against) my son in knee hockey in the basement. I haven't won a lot of things since I was in high school. You know, it elevates your career to a different level."

Defenseman Rob Scuderi, on the Penguins' journey from a first-round playoff exit in 2007, losing in the 2008 Final and winning the title this year:

"It's funny, you think about where we were a few years ago. We've come a long way with this core group. But at the end of the day, we all kind of expected this."

Winger Pascal Dupuis, on not having the words to describe his emotions:

"I never thought I'd be speechless. My wife can't believe it. But it's your dream coming true, so what can you say? That's the Stanley Cup, and I'm going to be on it."

Winger Chris Kunitz, on the Penguins' young stars Crosby and playoff MVP Evgeni Malkin:

"They're such emotional players. They are highly skilled, but they care so much about each other, and they'll do whatever it takes to be a part of it. Sid's got a bad knee, and he can barely skate, but he's on the bench trying to get just one shift. 'Geno' is throwing checks and playing defense all over the ice; that's the top scorer from the regular season and playoffs making smart plays because he knows the Cup is on the line. When your team has these young players, and they get it like that, it's rare. But so is a team like ours."

Defenseman Mark Eaton, on thousands of Penguins fans cheering them in Detroit for Game 7:

"This is unbelievable. When we scored that first goal, you could hear it. We looked at each other on the bench,

and it was weird. This is their building, but our fans were so loud. I'm not surprised. I've been in Pittsburgh for three years, and I can tell you that the fan support has been — unbelievable is the only word I can think of."

⚬⚬⚬⚬⚬

Winger Miroslav Satan, on winning the Cup three months after he was sent to the minors for salary-cap reasons:

"I can't believe this ending for me. If somebody would write a story in Hollywood about me this year and show it to me, I'd say, 'No, it can't happen.' I've waited a decade after losing (the 1999 Final) with Buffalo. I didn't think this could happen at the end of this year, but I kept going for that little chance. Just that little chance. It was worth it."

⚬⚬⚬⚬⚬

Senior hockey advisor Eddie Johnston, on the irony of the Penguins winning the Cup in front of former winger Marian Hossa, who opted to sign with Detroit last summer because he wanted to win a title:

"How do you like it that Satan raised the Cup ahead of Hossa? What Hossa did, I think it's unbelievable we came into his backyard and hoisted it, and he didn't. Poetic justice, I'd say."

⚬⚬⚬⚬⚬

Winger Matt Cooke, on the feel of the Cup:

"It's different than anything you imagine. The first time it felt like a feather. The second time it was heavier than I thought. But that first time — wow!"

⚬⚬⚬⚬⚬

Defenseman Kris Letang, on thinking of his late best friend Luc Boudron, who died in a motorcycle accident during the 2008 Final:

"(The Cup) was above my head, and I was thinking of just one person — Luc. This was for him from me."

⚬⚬⚬⚬⚬

CEO Ken Sawyer, who has been with the Penguins for 10 years, on that decade:

"It's so hard to describe. We've seen everything. Bankruptcy, trying to get the new arena, some seasons at the bottom of the standings — we've just been through everything. I've been involved in the NHL for 30 years, and this is my first time, and it's more special than I imagined. Can you believe that?"

⚬⚬⚬⚬⚬

Lemieux, on the past decade:

"It's been worthwhile all the way. We've gone through some very difficult times in Pittsburgh. That's how we got the draft picks that we got, finishing last every year. We made the decision to rebuild. It wasn't easy, but we went through it. It paid off tonight."

⚬⚬⚬⚬⚬

Assistant coach Tom Fitzgerald, on joining Bylsma's staff on Feb. 15:

"These guys right here (his children) have been away from me for four months. I told them, 'It could be two months, and it could be four months. And if it's four months, it's a great thing.' It's a great thing. It's a great thing."

⚬⚬⚬⚬⚬

Winger Bill Guerin, on his three months with the Penguins:

"(Receiving the Cup from Crosby) was amazing, and I appreciate the other guys giving me the opportunity to do that and just being able to be a big part of this team. I love 'em. They're great guys. This is a great team. When I got traded to Pittsburgh, the Pens were in 10th (place in the Eastern Conference). I was in 30th (overall with the Islanders), and the trade happened, and we all just started bonding together immediately and climbing the ladder."

⚬⚬⚬⚬⚬

Defenseman Hal Gill, on the Cup changing everything:

"We make good money, but this is why you play. It's different, I can't explain it. Until (Friday) afternoon, I never really knew how bad I wanted it. All you think about when it's right there is getting it done."

⚬⚬⚬⚬⚬

Defenseman Brooks Orpik, on turning down more money from other teams to re-sign with the Penguins last summer and having it pay off:

"This is why I came back. Maybe other people had their reasons to leave. But this is why I wanted to stay. ... I just didn't want to drop it. My legs were cramping up there, I thought I was going to buckle. It's a surreal moment, something you always dream about and something I went over in my head about 80 times the last couple days. You see other people doing it, but until you do it yourself, it's a completely different thing. It's better than you could ever imagine."

HUGE PITTSBURGH CROWD CELEBRATES THE PENGUINS' STANLEY CUP VICTORY

By Andrew Conte/TRIB TOTAL MEDIA

○ ○ ○ ○ ○

Tuesday, June 16, 2009

Throw a victory party for 375,000 fans on three days' notice?

Yeah, the City of Champions can handle that.

Penguins fans lined up 20 deep Monday along Grant Street and the Boulevard of the Allies to welcome back Lord Stanley's cup after a 17-year absence. Pittsburgh police estimated the 375,000 fans eclipsed by 25,000 the crowd who gathered four months ago to celebrate the Steelers' Super Bowl victory.

It was the third time in four years the city welcomed home a champion sports team.

"You deserve to be called the City of Champions," Penguins captain Sidney Crosby called out to the fans from a stage at Stanwix Street. "You deserve the Stanley Cup. Today is better than I ever dreamed, better than I think we all ever dreamed."

The crowd near the stage was packed in two hours before the noon start as fans bounced beach balls overhead and chanted, "Let's go Pens." Railings in parking garages along the parade route were lined with people above the sidewalk, and office workers wearing ties stood next to fans in black-and-gold T-shirts. The bells of First Lutheran Church on Grant Street rang as the team went by.

"Is this city unbelievable or what?" Penguins radio announcer Mike Lange called out from the stage.

Police arrested two people, and 23 were treated for heat-related medical problems.

The Penguins celebrated with temperatures in the upper 70s under skies as blue as the team's vintage, powder-blue sweaters.

The Pens' 2-1 victory Friday in Game 7 over the Detroit Red Wings might have come as a surprise to many who celebrated with the Vince Lombardi Trophy in February. Then, the Penguins stood at 10th place in the Eastern Conference, two slots away from even making the playoffs.

"This is a once-in-a-lifetime thing," said Ashleigh Munko, 21, of Moon, her voice hoarse from cheering and her fingernails painted half-black and half-gold with a thin white stripe in the middle. "You don't know if you'll ever get to see this again."

Team owner Mario Lemieux, the Hall-of-Famer who captained the past two Cup winners in 1991 and 1992, rode in a convertible to lead the parade. Players in white sweaters rode behind, standing on the backs of pickups next to wives, girlfriends and children.

The Cup is "right back where it belongs," Lemieux told the fans. "You guys are part of our family."

Center Evgeni Malkin rode with the Conn Smythe Trophy, which he won as the playoffs' most valuable player, and his parents, Vladimir and Natalia Malkin. Onstage, Malkin poured champagne into the cup and tilted it so his parents, who became celebrities as they cheered their son's team in recent weeks, could drink from it. Crosby then took a turn, holding the cup for his parents, Troy and Trina, to take a swig.

The victory party was a family event for spectators, too.

Angel Grossetti, 37, of New Brighton brought her five children — ranging in age from 14 to 4-year-old twins — along with one of their friends.

A sign on one stroller read, "I'm 6 months old, and I've already seen two championship parades."

Near the back of the crowd, Josh Herbert, 11, had gotten up before 6 a.m. to ride into Pittsburgh from his home in Columbiana, Ohio. At just 4 feet, 10 inches tall, he caught only glimpses of the parade when he stood on his tiptoes.

No matter, he said, "I can say, 'I was here.'"

Jasmine Goldband/Trib Total Media

Andrew Russell/Trib Total Media

Chaz Palla/Trib Total Med

Chaz Palla/Trib Total Media

Chaz Palla/Trib Total Media

"This is a chance of a lifetime to realize your childhood dream to win a Stanley Cup. Play without fear and you will be successful! See you at center ice."

— *Mario Lemieux, in a text message sent to each Penguins player on the morning of Game 7 of the Stanley Cup Final*